SUDDEN LEADERSHIP

A SURVIVAL GUIDE FOR PHYSICIANS

Malcolm Ogborn

"This book fills a niche that has been left mostly empty, until now. The practical and evidence-based content, the narratives, and the entertaining writing style make this a useful, easy to understand resource for the up-and-coming and early career physician-leader."

—**Dr John(y) Van Aerde, MD, MA(LT), PhD, FRCPC**
Executive Medical Director – Canadian Society of Physician Leaders

"'Sudden Leadership - A Survival Guide for Physicians' is an excellent resource on leadership in the health sector and beyond. It appeals to the reader at the introductory, intermediate and advanced levels based on their own lived experiences."

—**Dr. Roger Wong, CM, MD, FRCPC, FACP, FCAHS**
Vice Dean and Clinical Professor,
Faculty of Medicine, University of British Columbia

"This book is well written and referenced and would be a very valuable resource to any physician starting their leadership journey. I wish it had been available when I started mine. This book consolidates many aspects of leadership decisions and responsibility in a practical format in one place."

—**Dr Ken Harris, MD, FRCSC,**
Professor Emeritus,
Western University

 FriesenPress

One Printers Way
Altona, MB R0G 0B0
Canada

www.friesenpress.com

ISBN
978-1-03-913228-3 (Hardcover)
978-1-03-913227-6 (Paperback)
978-1-03-913229-0 (eBook)

1. Medical, Physicians

Distributed to the trade by The Ingram Book Company

For Jane

CONTENTS

FOREWORD

I am a coach. I mostly coach physicians, but sometimes other professionals find their way to me. Coaches aren't supposed to give advice, but I'm also a retired physician leader who has held leadership roles in clinical care and medical and health sciences research. Other physician leaders, particularly new ones, keep asking me for advice. This book is an attempt to resolve that conundrum. It's written from a physician viewpoint, but I suspect that any professional who must lead amongst highly qualified and often very independent peers will be able to relate to the examples used.

Writing a book for physician leaders may seem like an exercise for a very narrow market. That depends on how you define leadership. Most popular definitions reflect the idea that leaders influence and guide individuals and groups to achieve things. Those definitions do not include a requirement for a title, authority or formal qualifications. Neither does this book. Whether it is supporting patient and families through medical complexity, doing a small quality improvement project, running a clinic or department, or overseeing a facility or an entire healthcare system, leading is something all physicians are likely to do in some way, and at some time in their career. This purpose of this book is to help physicians be ready in those moments.

There are now many excellent resources to support and train physician leaders who do take on more formal leadership roles. Imagine if we lived in a world where physicians made an early career choice that they wanted to lead. They would then enter a clear career pathway that provided incremental training in proportion to needs of steadily increasing leadership responsibilities. They'd have time to participate in the available excellent training relevant to their needs before they needed to apply those skills and knowledge, or at least, just in time. For most physician leaders, this career path remains a distant hope rather than a reality. My coaching clients usually come to leadership down one of two pathways. The most common is that a senior or respected colleague taps them on the shoulder to take on the role. That role is often already vacant or about to become so. This happens more often during crisis points for organizations or parts thereof. There's little or no time for preparation for the role. The other path is taken when someone becomes sufficiently passionate about a cause to step up to try to make a difference. They're armed with passion but poorly prepared for the process. In both cases, they are dedicated, passionate people who usually take on the leadership role while continuing to do the same amount of clinical care, teaching, and research, while also juggling a life outside of medicine. With six months' notice, on a good day, assuming no one else in the department or their family has a crisis and there aren't any unexpected budget cuts, they might get to one leadership course per year. If that describes your lot, this book is written for you.

Helping clients explore for resources and ideas that will help them excel falls within the mandate of a coach. There are challenges doing this with physician leaders. Physician leaders often have limited time to dedicate to research about leadership. They also often need these different skills urgently. Although physicians are highly educated and better trained in the use of literature than most people, they live in a narrowly focused academic world. Although this is changing slowly, most of the high quality, evidence-based leadership-practice research literature exists outside the health sphere. This is not a road well travelled by physicians. The final challenge is that physicians are bred and trained to be skeptics. They prefer resources supported by empirical proof.

I'm commonly asked, *"Is there somewhere where introductory physician leader stuff is all in one place?"* If there is, I have yet to find it. Think of this book as the travel guide you might buy before a major trip. It provides some suggested itineraries around common challenges. It covers some of the background and details that you might find along the way. It points you in the direction of other resources that might be helpful and of interest. This book is not a deep treatise on leadership theory. No disrespect is intended to the deep wisdom that exists in these many frameworks. You'll find many of them listed in the "Further Reading" sections. Everything listed in those sections was, at the time of writing, accessible through online book shops or online academic library services that most physicians other high-level professionals should be able to access.

The order of the topics in the book is deliberate. It reflects the most common sequence of concerns that new leaders have presented to me in coaching and workshop sessions. I have tried to write each chapter so that it can stand alone as a reference in time of need. This means you can choose to read the book cover to cover, or cherry pick chapters that meet your immediate needs. If you do the latter, I would still encourage you to read and reflect upon the first two chapters first; understanding your own vision of leadership and the skills of engaging with others underpin almost everything else.

This book is about leadership tactics rather than theory; it's a manual of things physician leaders can actually do to work with the common conundrums they face. I touch on some of the theory behind these practices, but I do so lightly. My goal is to provide physician leaders with some tools to use right from the start of their leadership. This book will not take you straight to the mastery of leadership, but if it helps you to experience some early satisfaction and success, and that in turn stimulates you to engage deeper, I will be delighted. This book is about "how." "Why" is another journey for you.

I have used and coached with everything in this book in the service of medical leadership. Consider everything field tested. There are some areas that physician leaders find challenging that are not included. Finance and contracts do fall within the sphere of operations of some physician leaders, but working with these often involves very detailed and specific processes that are unique to the organization involved. Rather than sow confusion, I urge you to seek organizational support for these situations. Negotiation is mentioned briefly in the chapter on Conflict, but if this is to be a major part of your role, I strongly encourage you to both read deeper and complement that reading with training by negotiation specialists. Many of the concepts introduced are supported by specific intensive training programs that you may find useful if those models resonate with you.

This book is not an alternative to coaching. Discussions around application of the practices described here are good starting points for both informal and formal coaching conversations. Awareness of the value of coaching to leadership and subsequently to organizational quality is growing in the physician leadership world. Application of that awareness to structure, policy, and practice still has some way to go before access to this type of support is as widely available to physician leaders as it is in most other high-technology, high-performance environments. I hope you will explore the benefits coaching can offer your leadership.

Good luck and smooth sailing on your leadership journey!

SUDDEN LEADERSHIP

OUR CAST

This book is going to follow the initial journey and challenges of two new, but imaginary medical leaders. You'll meet them as they face issues that are commonly experienced by physicians who take up the leadership mantle. While the characters are fictional, their circumstances and conundrums are almost certainly going to resemble those of "anyone living or dead" to some degree. Great pains have been taken, however, not to draw on any complete, individual real-life situations. Scenarios have been synthesized from elements of many, many physician-leadership and physician-leadership-coaching encounters. If you think you see yourself or someone close to you in the story, it really is coincidence!

Rosalind is a thirty-eight-year-old emergency physician who has just taken on the role of Chief of Staff at a hospital in a small rural city. The hospital has seventy-two beds with specialist support in Anesthesia, General Surgery, Internal Medicine, Obstetrics, Psychiatry, and Pediatrics. Some visiting subspecialists also hold privileges. The nearest tertiary facility is about four hundred kilometres away, so the hospital often confronts challenging clinical situations as the first line of care. Rosalind had served as the head of the Emergency Department for a bit over two years prior to taking this role.

She took that position a year after arriving in the community with her partner, Susan, after a stint in Africa with Medicin Sans Frontiers. She and Susan, who is a freelance web-designer and digital-marketing specialist, love the lifestyle of the region, have bought a small ranch, and are exploring options to start a family. Rosalind is passionate about healthcare equity and finding ways to improve services to marginalized groups in society. She is well liked by ER staff and many of the younger physicians but has experienced some friction with some of the senior medical staff members, particularly when she has felt they've been dismissive or not adequately responsive to ER situations and requests.

Rosalind took the position after it had been vacant for several months after the previous incumbent developed a serious illness precluding a return to work. She accepted the position with some reservations but at the urging of the regional executive medical director. Although she was the only candidate, she was interviewed by a search committee consisting of both medical staff and administrative representatives, and it's rumoured that she received a majority, but not unanimous, recommendation.

Sanjay is a thirty-nine-year-old Internal Medicine specialist with additional certification in addictions medicine. He has just been appointed department head of medicine at an urban community hospital. The 220-bed community hospital has no formal subspecialty medical departments. He has twenty-three department members consisting of thirteen internal medicine specialists who do general medicine and some ICU call, four cardiologists working a separate call schedule, four physical medicine specialists, a solo endocrinologist, and a solo rheumatologist. The department is hoping to set up a gastroenterology group one day.

Sanjay and his wife, Evelyn, have two school-age children who are very active academically, in sports, and in music. Evelyn works four days per week as a social worker with an agency helping women offenders. He also has extensive extended family connections within the local Tamil community, including his aging immigrant parents who have some chronic health programs. Keeping his family connected to that origin is important to him.

He is passionate about providing high quality, evidence-based care. He likes to work by building consensus, and he's popular with non-medical staff, medical students, and rotating residents. He's had some frustration with perceived administrative barriers to care, and at one point, he was referred to work with a mediator around some harsh words with a site director.

Sanjay was asked to take the role by the Chief of Staff. There was no formal search beyond the Chief of Staff asking if there were any objections at a department meeting, and again inviting opinions from department members in an email. In compliance with the medical staff bylaws, the appointment was recommended by the hospital Medical Advisory Committee without discussion and subsequently confirmed by the Board.

WHY AM I LEADING?

Rosalind comes into an 8:00 a.m. to 4:00 p.m. day shift the day after the announcement of her appointment as Chief of Staff, effective in about two weeks, was sent out to all medical and hospital staff. Throughout the morning, staff in the ER congratulate her on her new appointment and wish her well. While waiting in line at the coffee shop, one of the senior internal medicine specialists stops as he passes her. Raising an eyebrow, he says. "So, you're to be our new Chief, are you?"

"I am," Rosalind replies, "starting in two weeks. I think I'm looking forward to it and dreading it at the same time!"

"Well, I guess we'll see if you can last longer than the last one. It's not really a job for a ... millennial," he replies, walking away without waiting for a response.

Rosalind is a bit taken aback, but it's not her first prickly encounter with that physician, so she tries to brush it off.

Later in the day, at the end of her shift, she hands over to a colleague whom she considers a friend.

"Rosalind, I didn't know you had applied for the COS job. Why did you do that? The old-fart brigade here will make your life hell. Why not just keep your head down and leave the politics to someone else—you're too nice for that job."

This is not the vote of confidence for which she had hoped. When Rosalind gets home, Susan takes one look at her and asks, "What's wrong?"

Rosalind frowns. "Am I making a big mistake taking the Chief of Staff job?"

Susan smiles. "I think we need a glass of wine for this conversation"

Choosing to lead

"Why become a physician leader?"

If you ask that question in public, you'll hear lots of excellent justifications for having physicians in leadership positions. Having healthcare led by people with a deep understanding of the nature and challenges of clinical work is a proven asset in improving the quality of care. Having the groups involved in the delivery of care represented in leadership is useful in engaging with these groups (we talk more about this later). Numerous articles list reasons why physicians *should* take up leadership roles, but not so many discuss why they *do*. All well and good for the system, but what's in it for you? Let's rephrase the question:

"Why do you feel the need to become a physician leader?"

The distinguished physician leader Dr. Ruth Collins-Nakai once wrote: "Many physicians can truly be considered 'accidental leaders.'" Physician leaders often characterize their leadership start as being asked by someone to "step up." The "tap on the shoulder" as a common entry point to leadership, rather than following a logical career path, is supported by research findings. In a study of nurses and doctors who moved to leadership positions, Dr. Ivan Spehar and colleagues at the University of Oslo found that while most went through a period of increasing awareness that there was more that they could do or be, the actual tipping point to moving into a position was often a conversation with a superior or colleague. Some physicians talk of feeling that they have a duty to contribute. Sometimes, circumstances such as a health condition or family commitments require a shift away from a previous role. These answers are still skirting the issue. The important question, the answer to which will shape your approach to leadership, is this: What made you say yes to the leadership opportunity when you could have said no. If you keep picking away at this, most physician leaders eventually say something like:

"I <u>need</u> to make a difference."

There is a story that, in 1961, John F. Kennedy was visiting NASA head-quarters for the first time. He introduced himself to a janitor and asked him what his role was at NASA. The janitor replied, "I'm helping put a man on the moon." The moral of this is that someone created a strong and specific purpose at that time for everybody in NASA. What is your purpose? Can you describe the difference you want to make? Let's try a little exercise. Complete the following statement:

I will make a difference as a leader by _____.

<insert your purpose, the main thing(s) you hope to achieve here>

Now, let's explore why you need to make a difference. Dr. Åsa Lindgren and colleagues at the University of Gothenburg interviewed physicians to explore their interest and motivation in health system development. They found that physicians committed to system development who "wanted to make a difference" expressed a strong theme of feeling useful and making progress, which they characterized as professional fulfill-ment. This fits well with predictions of a model of human motivation called Self Determination Theory. This field of psychology, based upon work by Drs Edward Deci and Richard Ryan, holds that we have innate needs to grow, develop, and change, just as we have innate needs toward sustenance, safety, and reproduction. We shape our sense of ourselves through three areas: autonomy, competence, and relatedness. Autonomy is our need to feel in control of ourselves and what we seek to achieve. Competence speaks to our need to demonstrate mastery of skills and processes. Relatedness is about our need to belong within groups and to feel connected or attached to others.

You can use these three headings to gain insight into why you are seeking a leadership role and where you might focus your efforts to improve both your leadership and your comfort level within the role. Whether you're in a leadership role or considering one, try this exercise:

Write down answers to the following questions:

1. How does/will this role increase my control in achieving my goals? (Autonomy)

   _____

2. What does/would need to change for me to feel more in control in achieving my goals? (Autonomy)

   _____

3. What skills and talents does/would this role allow me to practise and demonstrate? (Competence)

   _____

4. What skills do I need to improve or acquire to perform this role? (Competence)

   _____

5. What connections does/will this role create or enable for me, and what connections might it jeopardize? (Relatedness)

   _____

6. What connections do I need to establish to be effective in this role and which might I have to change? (Relatedness)

   _____

I often use these questions in coaching conversations with clients who are thinking about taking a new position. The answers to the odd-numbered questions speak to why you are looking at the role. You might want to consider whether your answers can help you assess, over time, how much the role is a success for you personally. The even-numbered questions are a good place to start planning activities that will help your leadership be more enjoyable and effective by setting some specific goals and timelines.

Leading with Values

There is another layer on top of needs that exerts a powerful influence on choice and style in leadership. That layer is values. Values can show up at different levels. Outrage at a perceived unfairness, concern for avoidable suffering, or an aspiration for excellence may have been the trigger that pushed you into acting on a need for autonomy, competence, and relatedness. The desire to see a kinder, more considerate workplace may be important to you. Being able to show pride in your standard of care may urge you on.

Table 1. Examples of Values

Adventure	Contribution	Happiness	Optimism
Achievement	Compassion	Harmony	Peace
Authenticity	Courage	Honesty	Popularity
Autonomy	Creativity	Humility	Realism
Balance	Curiosity	Humour	Recognition
Boldness	Determination	Integrity	Safety
Compassion	Fairness	Justice	Self Respect
Challenge	Faith	Kindness	Self Love
Family	Friendship	Learning	Service
Citizenship	Fun	Loyalty	Spirituality
Community	Grace	Modesty	Trustworthiness
Competency	Growth	Openness	

This list is based on values identified in conversations with physicians but is not exhaustive.

Once in a leadership role, values shape how you behave and how you would like to be seen. Leaders are often expected to demonstrate the stated values of their organization. Conflict between personal and organizational values has been proposed as a driver of workplace stress and burnout in areas outside of healthcare, although publications report conflicting findings. Irrespective of the alignment with the organization, finding success and satisfaction in leadership rests heavily on knowing and being faithful to personal values while securing achievements that are meaningful to you.

Try this exercise.

1. Write down your most important values (five to ten). You can use Table 1 to help or do the free online assessment at the Barrett Values Centre (https://www.valuescentre.com/tools-assessments/pva/).

   _____

2. Write down the published values of the organization for which you have/are considering a leadership role.

   _____

3. For the values that you share with the organization, list some ways you can demonstrate them in your leadership.

   _____

   _____

   _____

4. For personal values that are not on the organizational list (if any), list some ways you can demonstrate those values without conflicting with the organization's values.

   _____

   _____

5. For organizational values that are not on your personal list (if any), list some ways you can demonstrate those values without conflicting with your personal values

_____

_____

_____

Setting Leadership Goals

Now you have a defined purpose. It's likely that you're working in an organization that also has a mission, vision, and goals. These words, and the activities that generate them, frequently produce eye rolling when raised with physician leaders, or any leaders. Sadly, that's probably a reflection of either how poorly these things are generated, or how organizations fail to live up to them, diminishing their significance and meaning. Eye rolling aside, your leadership journey will be clearer if you have a vision and goals in addition to purpose. Let me a use a metaphor to illustrate these terms:

You have decided to visit India. All your life, you've been intrigued by the varied and spectacular buildings that exist there. Your mission is to experience and learn about the architecture and history of India. Your vision is how you describe what you expect to experience and what it will feel like (i.e., the actual sensory experience). Your goals can be "process goals," such as creating a different way of doing something, like learning how to travel and get around using public transport in India. They can be "outcome goals," in which you achieve a specific measurable result, such as visiting the Taj Mahal in Agra and Meenakshi Amman Temple in Madurai.

If you haven't already, you'll encounter the term "SMART goals" in your leadership journey. This useful tool arose from the writings of George Doran in 1981. While the acronym has become immensely popular, his original model, which was aimed at managers setting goals for subordinates, has changed somewhat over the years. The most popular version, popularized by Paul Meyer and based on a 2001 essay published by Professor Robert Rubin, is as follows:

Specific—It should be very clear what the goal is.

Measurable—You need some objective way or metric that will confirm when the goal is met.

Achievable—The goal may be challenging or a stretch, but it should be possible. In the original model, this stood for "assignable," meaning you could identify to whom the goal was given.

Relevant—Achieving this goal supports your mission/ purpose and brings your vision closer to reality. In the original model, this was "realistic," now supplanted by achievable above.

Time-bound—A time frame can be realistically set to achieve the goal.

Try this exercise. Think of either a process or outcome goal(s) for your leadership and set them up under the SMART framework:

Specific (articulate exactly what will be achieved)

_____

Measurable (What measure will you use to know the goal is achieved?)

_____

Achievable (What enables this goal to be achieved [e.g., personnel, resources, regulatory environment, space, etc.]?)

_____

Relevant (How does it contribute to your purpose/mission, and vision?)

_____

Time bound (When will it be done?)

_____

Setting goals should come with a disclaimer, and here it is: If you sit down right now and set goals, you'll be doing so based largely on what you're experiencing in the moment. But say the world suddenly changes tomorrow ... because it always does. Is your goal still relevant? In pursuing this goal, are you ignoring something more important? If you use goals, it's important to put aside a few minutes every week or month to reflect on them. By reflection, I mean more than just checking the milestones. I mean re-asking every one of the SMART questions again. A good leader can take their team in a specific direction but also has the flexibility to change direction and let goals go when that's the right thing to do. Good communication with your team around such changes is critical. Your goals should be a useful guide, not an overbearing master. The excellent review by Lisa Ordóñez in the "Further Reading" section at the end of this chapter gives an excellent appraisal of the limitations of goals.

My Personal Leadership Statement

Now let's take all three of these exercises and write a personal leadership statement.

> "I have taken on this leadership role to be better able to *<enter your purpose>*. This role will better enable me to achieve these goals by *<enter ways in which autonomy is enhanced>*. I bring *<enter existing talent/skills to the role>* and will strive to develop *<enter new required or desired talents/ skills>*. I will work to develop new relationships with/within

> *<enter new relationships made possible or required by the role>* while taking care to maintain *<enter existing valued relationships>*. While leading, I will demonstrate *<enter personal value>* by *<enter behaviour that exemplifies it; repeat for each value as needed>*."

While framing this and putting it on your wall may be a bit extreme, if that works for you, go for it! At least keep it somewhere accessible and make regular appointments with yourself, perhaps every three months or so, to spend thirty to sixty minutes re-reading it, reflecting on how you are doing, and updating if necessary.

Boundaries

Another important area that needs reflection and definition are your boundaries as a leader. This term has long been used in clinical practices with a narrow and specific meaning around maintaining proper, objective relationships with clients/patients. The revelations of the #MeToo movement have reinforced this type of boundary concept in many other domains. But boundaries have other important applications in leadership. Think of leadership as a complicated object that can be seen in different dimensions. In each dimension, it has an edge where it ends and something else begins. That is the boundary for that dimension.

Researcher, author, and consultant Dr. Brené Brown talks of defining personal boundaries for leaders: "setting boundaries is making clear what's okay, and what's not okay, and why." It's important to find the edges on what behaviours and actions are and are not acceptable in your landscape. Brown advocates that knowing this and sharing it is of great value in developing trust-based relationships and allowing leaders to work with their own vulnerabilities.

Dr. Gervase Bushe, another researcher, author, and consultant, views boundaries from the lens of needing to define the edges of one's personal experience, the final construct in our minds that is generated by sensory input and cognitive and emotional processing. He advocates that effective leadership is supported by clarity on the leader's own experience and what belongs to other people. If we are clear on what's being generated in our own heads and can differentiate that from the experience of others, while striving to understand and appreciate the alternate experience, we're in a better leadership position. He argues that we should avoid allowing ourselves to be ruled, positively or negatively, by the experience of others, a state he calls "fused," when the boundary around our own experience is too leaky.

Examples of this could include acting to keep someone happy or to keep them away to save us ourselves anxiety over what they're experiencing, rather than acting from what we believe should happen. On the other hand, being rendered completely impervious to the experience of others by a hard, impenetrable boundary around our experience—a state he calls "disconnected"—is also to be avoided. An example would be implementing a change that will adversely affect another person or group, without even being aware of or considering the implications for them. An appropriate differentiated leadership response would be to not let the impact on them stop a necessary change but to sympathize with their plight and explore reasonable mitigation strategies. Dr. Henry Cloud, a psychologist and consultant who has written several best-selling books specifically about boundaries and boundary setting in personal and professional life, makes the comment that as leaders, "you get what you create and what you allow."[1] What will you allow?

Boundary setting develops with time and should retain some flexibility as people and circumstances change. A full discussion of the mechanism of setting boundaries is beyond the scope of this book; my point in this section is to get you thinking about yours. That said, there is no time like the present to start. Can you list a few things you will allow in your leadership and a few that you won't, both within your behaviour and thoughts and the behaviour of those around you? Can you test when you're doing something based on your experience and when you're reacting to

---

1 Henry Cloud, *Boundaries for Leaders: Results, Relationships and Being Ridiculously in Charge* (New York: HarperCollins, 2013): 14.

someone else's? Can you think of a time when you disregarded someone else's experience that, on reflection, warranted your attention?

Reasons to Not Accept a Leadership Role

Are there poor reasons for taking leadership roles? For most physicians, adopting leadership roles does not enhance material rewards; indeed, it might have the reverse effect, so purely mercenary motives are usually off the table. Seeking authority to make something happen may be a wish. In fact, while the type of power that comes with a title may be useful in transiently enforcing compliance to policy, it tends to be a poor tool for system change. Authority does not change minds and hearts. Changing process without changing minds is a recipe for resistance and sabotage. We will explore this in more detail in a later chapter. This isn't to say that a leadership role doesn't offer opportunities for influence and profound change. Such influence, however, arises from the enhanced relationship opportunities that a good leadership position presents.

Enhancing status and respect may work as a reason in some situations, but the community of physicians doesn't tend to put its leaders on pedestals; indeed, working in leadership for healthcare organizations is often described as "going to the dark side" by the physician community. Assume respect is earned, not conferred.

Taking a leadership role under pressure from someone else to serve their agenda can be a pathway to a very unhappy time if their goals and needs aren't closely aligned with yours. Although it's true that others may see potential in us that we underappreciate ourselves, it's important to distinguish between encouragement to take a position for your sake, the action of a friend, or for their sake—the action of a manipulator.

Taking a role to block someone else from getting it, whether on your own initiative or at the behest of others, is usually a mistake. If there are no suitable candidates for a position, there are more constructive ways of finding interim solutions while the question of why no suitable person applied is properly considered. Blocking as a strategy usually guarantees at least one very unhappy individual.

Perhaps the worst reason for taking a leadership role, but one that is surprisingly common among physicians, is that it's "your turn." Leadership is not dishwashing, and leadership selection should be more discriminating than passing the hair shirt. Accidental leadership can be a happy accident; truly reluctant leadership rarely is.

Whatever the path that puts a leadership role in front of you, run through the questions listed in this chapter. If you can't find a satisfying answer to them, it's time to question whether this is the role or the time for you. Saying no to such an opportunity is a tough, anxiety-provoking conversation that will call for courage, but the cost of a wrong decision is inevitably higher. I will cover techniques to help with this type of conversation in a later chapter.

Let's check in on Rosalind and Susan ...

Susan tops up the chardonnay. "So, we've established that this job will help you introduce some of your quality improvement ideas in other departments. It will also give you a more official standing to build on the conversations you've started with community groups about getting their input about hospital programs. Right?"

Rosalind smiles. "Right, as usual, Ms. Analytical Mind!"

Susan raises her glass in acknowledgement. "So, tell me why this is better than what you can do now."

"Well, I can get a ... higher viewpoint. I mean, see things at a level above just the links between the ER and the wards. I'll be more involved in recruitment and perhaps able to both lift our image and make sure we're recruiting people for what the hospital needs rather than just individual practices. I may be able to finally get some community people on our committees. I'm looking forward to applying some of the things I learned in those leadership courses about engaging people and passing on some of the quality improvement training. I'm also looking forward to getting to connect more with the docs who don't spend a lot of time in the ER and meeting more of the staff

without someone being resuscitated between us. And, of course, I'll now be able to officially do some of the community work."

Susan is nodding. "Sounds good. But what's the catch? Or should I say, the catches?"

Rosalind thinks for a moment. "Well, at a personal level, there's no way of pretending this isn't more work. If we as a couple aren't going to pay a price for that, I need to convince the ER group to change shift scheduling, and maybe even recruit, so that I have enough time to do this properly. I know I haven't always made friends by trying to champion the ER. I'll need to work on taking a deep breath and listening, including to some people who make me want to head out the nearest door. I guess I am their Chief of Staff too."

"Fair enough, but how will you do all that?"

"I think the first thing I need to do is set up a meeting with Jim (the regional Executive Medical Director) with a bit of a formal agenda. I think his support will be helpful in dealing with the ER group and persuading them that losing a bit of my billing will be offset by having me better connected to leadership. I'm also going to need someone I can bounce things off at pretty short notice at first. Maybe him, maybe someone else who's been in a similar position for a longer time, or maybe both. I'd like to connect with others doing this type of work as well in other communities, since I'm the only one here. And I'm hoping they'll pay for some more leadership training or coaching."

Susan raises her glass again. "Sounds like a plan!"

Key Learnings

- *Leadership is a choice. Know why you have chosen it.*

- *To enjoy leadership, it must meet your needs as well as those you lead. Pay particular attention to how it will allow you to demonstrate competence, achieve autonomy, and develop new relationships.*

- *Identify an overall purpose for your leadership.*

- *Set SMART goals for your leadership but hold them lightly and be flexible when circumstances change.*

- *Know and share the values that guide your leadership.*

- *Have the courage to decline a leadership role if the choice does not feel right.*

FURTHER READING

Choosing to Lead

John Byrnes, "The Value of Physician Leaders," *Journal of Healthcare Management,* 61(2016): 251–255.

Ruth Collins-Nakai, "Leadership in Medicine," *McGill Journal of Medicine,* 9(2006): 68–73.

Jean-Louis Denis and Nicolette van Gestel, "Medical Doctors in Healthcare Leadership: Theoretical and Practical Challenges," *BMC Health Services Research,* 16, Suppl 1 (2016): 45–56.

David E. Stein and Lauren D'Innocenzo, "So, You Want to Be a Leader?" *Seminars in Colon and Rectal Surgery* (In Press), 2021. https://doi.org/10.1016/j.scrs.2021.100810.

Ivan Spehar, Jan C. Frich, and Lars Erik Kjekshus, "Clinicians' Experience of Becoming a Clinical Manager: A Qualitative Study," *BMC Health Services Research,* 12(2012): 421–432.

Richard M. Ryan, R.M. and Edward L. Deci, *Self-Determination Theory: Basic Psychological Needs in Motivation, Development, and Wellness* (New York: The Guilford Press, 2017).

Åsa Lindgren, Fredrik Bååthe, and Lotta Dellve, "Why Risk Professional Fulfilment: A Grounded Theory of Physician Engagement in Healthcare Development," *International Journal of Health Planning and Management,* 28(2013): e138-e157.

Leading with Values

Barrett Values Centre, "Personal Values Assessment. Understanding Your Values," August 1, 2021, https://www.valuescentre.com/tools-assessments/pva/.

Carol P. Herbert, "Perspectives in Primary Health Care: Values-Driven Leadership is Essential in Health Care," *Annals of Family Medicine,* 13(2015): 512–513.

Setting Leadership Goals

Mindtools Content Team, "SMART Goals. How to Make Your Goals Achievable," August 1· 2021, https://www.mindtools.com/pages/article/smart-goals.htm.

Lisa D. Ordóñez, Maurice E. Schweitzer, Adam D. Galinsky, and Max H. Bazerman, "Goals Gone Wild: The Systematic Side Effects of Overprescribing Goal Setting," *Academy of Management Perspectives,* 23(2009): 6–16.

Boundaries

Brené Brown, *Dare to Lead* (New York: Random House, 2018).

Gervase R. Bushe, *Clear Leadership: Sustaining Real Collaboration and Partnership at Work* (Boston: Davies-Black, 2010).

Henry Cloud, *Boundaries for Leaders: Results, Relationships and Being Ridiculously in Charge* (New York: HarperCollins, 2013).

IF I'M LEADING,
WHO IS FOLLOWING?

Sanjay decides to start his tenure as a department head with a meet and greet to introduce the ideas he'd like to bring to the department. He picks a Thursday evening at 5:00 p.m. as the time and arranges for pizza, salad, and soft drinks to be delivered to the hospital boardroom. He sends out invitations to all department members two weeks before the event and sends reminders a week before and the day before. He spends hours perfecting a PowerPoint presentation of his ideas and agenda.

The day arrives. To Sanjay's dismay, by 5.30 p.m., only four people out of the twenty-three invited have turned up. Three are the physicians with whom he shares a private office practice and one, rather to his surprise, is Gwen, their sole endocrinologist. Gwen has a well-earned reputation for not being shy in pointedly expressing her opinions. She had openly expressed reservations about his ability at the previous department meeting when his appointment was announced. She was department head for over ten years some time back. Feeling rather sheepish, Sanjay goes ahead with his presentation. His practice partners applaud and make suggestions for how he might polish the presentation. Gwen, who has been uncharacteristically quiet, then speaks up.

"What makes you think this is what anybody else in the department wants? Have you asked them?"

Sanjay is stung. "Pretty hard to ask them when they're not here!"

"And why is that?" Gwen replies.

Sanjay shrugs, feeling a bit humiliated.

The meeting quickly fizzles, and the large amount of left-over food and drink is distributed by the attendees to the very busy ER and ICU staff.

The next morning, Sanjay spots Christine, the Chief of Staff, at the coffee shop and asks to talk. They find a table, and Sanjay immediately begins to unload about his apathetic and disinterested department members. Christine listens without interrupting. When Sanjay finally comes up for air, she thinks for a second and then looks straight at Sanjay.

"Sanjay, your department members, are they competent physicians?"

"Well, yeah."

"Do you think they're basically smart people?"

"Yeah, they are."

"Do you think they're concerned about providing good medical care?"

"On the whole, yes."

"Does that fit with what you vented just now?"

Sanjay pauses. "Not really, I guess."

Christine smiles. "Don't beat yourself up too much. Leading your department has never been particularly easy. But let's stop making this about the people. Let's focus on this as an issue of how these generally good physicians behave when they're asked to engage with the department as a group and you as the leader."

Followership

It seems obvious that having followers is part of the definition of leadership. In times and situations where leaders led by simple authority, the role of followers didn't get much attention. While well-quoted literature on leadership goes back centuries or millennia to the times of Machiavelli and even Sun Tzu, the literature on followership has only recently begun to achieve popularity. Physician leaders often have limited authority over the physicians they lead. This limits for them the utility of concepts coming from rigid hierarchies with steep power gradients between the leaders and the led. Physician leaders must often succeed with influence and charisma alone, rather than authority. They need a clear understanding of the behaviour, needs, and loyalty of their followers.

The modern focus on followership emerged with the publication by Robert Kelley of an article in 1988 in the *Harvard Business Review*: "In Praise of Followers." Four years later, he published his influential book, *The Power of Followership: How to Create Leaders People Want to Follow and Followers Who Lead Themselves*. Kelley proposed that followers fall into five categories based on where they fall on two axes. The first is a spectrum of passive to active behaviour toward the goals of the organization/leader. The second ranges from dependent through to being independent, which is characterized by the demonstration of critical thinking (Figure 1).

The resulting followership categories are *Passive, Exemplary, Alienated, Conformist, and Pragmatist*. Those who are neither active nor independent are Passive. They do as they're told but nothing more. Those at the opposite pole on both are Exemplary. They take the initiative and demonstrate originality and creativity in pursuit of the leader's goals. Kelley's original work saw the proportion of Exemplary followers as key to success. Those who are independent but inactive are the Alienated, and as the title suggests, their behaviour may involve criticism without involvement in improvement. Conformists are active in pursuit of organizational goals if direction is provided but will accomplish little if left to their own initiative. Those who are mid range in both axes are the Pragmatists, sometime called pragmatic survivors, who may go with the flow but can lean toward or away from effectiveness at different times. Although it has been recently proposed as a framework for surgical followership, fitting Kelley's model to all physician leadership can be problematic.

Independent, critical thinking

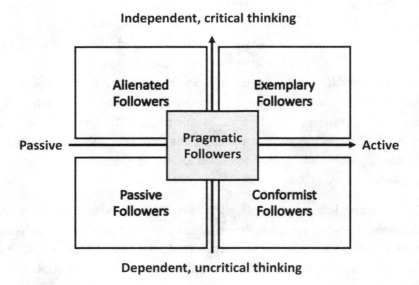

Figure 1. Kelley's model of followership. (Adapted from Kelley, R. E. [1992]. The power of followership)

Physicians' roles are complex, and their behaviour in different dimensions, such as in direct patient care versus participating in departmental quality activities, may be quite different. The action arising out of Kelley's model is often referred to as "developing" followers along the activity and independence axes. This level of direction of personal development may be beyond the practical influence many leaders have within physician and medical staff groups who are associates and peers rather than employees.

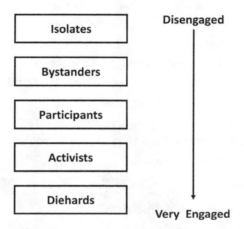

Figure 2. Kellerman's model of followership (adapted from Kellerman, B, Harvard Business Review [2007, December]).

In 2008, Barbara Kellerman also published a *Harvard Business Review* article and a book on followership: *Followership: How Followers Are Creating Change and Changing Leaders*. She also divided followers into five groups: *Isolates, Bystanders, Participants, Activists*, and *Diehards*. Isolates are disconnected from their leaders; they keep their heads down and do what they see as their role with little regard to the organization within which they work. Bystanders remain aware of their leaders and the organization but choose not to engage. Participants will contribute but aren't strongly committed to the leader. They may drift in another direction if they don't agree with a direction the leader is taking. Activists have strong feelings about their role, their leaders, and the organization. They can be engaged and strong supporters or very active opponents, depending on their stance on an issue. Diehards will go to any length in a cause in which they are invested. They'll sacrifice everything in defence of a leader whom they support, or they'll take the leader down with them if they oppose them. The important feature of Kellerman's typology of followership is that the classification is based upon only one dimension— the level of engagement of the follower. Securing or reinforcing physician engagement is something physician leaders can and should do. Linking followership to engagement makes a lot of sense in the physician world.

It is very important to remember that the terms *follower* or *leader* describe what is someone is doing, not who they are. Someone who leads in one aspect of an organization or situation, will be a follower in another aspect. How that leader publicly models follower behaviour may be a powerful influence on their own followers. Bluntly put, if you want good followers, be one. In some situations, the most effective approach may be for a leader to promote one of their own followers who are adequately qualified, and follow themselves. I touch on this more when we discuss team development.

Credibility

If the role of a leader is to influence or guide, people need to believe you. What makes a leader credible? An awful lot has been written on the characteristics of successful leaders. The lists vary in length, but confidence, competence, decisiveness, optimism, empathy, and good communication skills are on most of them. If being these things is important, what do you as leader do to be seen as having these properties? While physician-specific studies are lacking, Daniel Han Ming Chng, Tae-Yeol Kim, Brad Gilbreath, and Lynne Andersson collaborated in a number of studies of different types of US workers and students to explore this question. They confirmed that followers assessed their leader's credibility in two main dimensions: competence and trustworthiness. They noted that followers tended to emphasize positive information in competence but were more likely to be biased toward negative information in trustworthiness. They asked their subjects to rank specific leadership behaviours, rather than personal characteristics, that either reinforced or diminished perceptions of competence and trustworthiness. These findings are summarized in Table 2.

Table 2.

Competent leaders ...	Trustworthy leaders ...
Emphasize the future	Communicate and act with consistency
Emphasize group/organizational outcomes	Protect the group and its members
Emphasize group members and	Embody the group/organization's vision
their contributions	and values
Take action and show initiative	Consult and listen to stakeholders
Communicate well	Communicate openly
Participate in learning relevant to their leadership	Show they value group members
	Support group members and stakeholders

Incompetent leaders ...	Untrustworthy leaders ...
Fail to appear adequately knowledgeable	Promote or engage in unethical behaviour
Fail to act	Lie
Act to reinforce their own egos	Act for their own benefit rather the group's
Sow confusion	Behave inconsistently
Communicate poorly	Communicate guardedly or overcautiously
Are not open to other viewpoints	Ignore others' input
	Treat group members as expendable

Behaviours That Influence Perception of Leadership Credibility (adapted from Chng, D.H.M et al, MIT Sloan Management Review)

Behaviours that promote credibility aren't always simply the opposite of behaviours that erode it. Also, one good behaviour does not simply cancel out one bad one. Research in cognitive psychology consistently finds that negative experiences have a bigger impact than positive ones. If you look at the list above, you'll notice that the behaviours that influence trustworthiness are more about how a leader is personally experienced by followers. Our brain is always on heightened alert for negative experience, so this accounts for the negative bias we must overcome when looking at trustworthiness information.

Try this exercise. For the first part, make two columns on a sheet of paper. Look at the list of positive behaviours in Table 2 and then write one or two specific things you currently do or could do in the context of your leadership role that demonstrates that behaviour. For the second part, reach out to a trusted person and give them the list of negative behaviours and ask them to suggest any examples of things you do that might fall into one of those behaviours. Be prepared to take this feedback in the spirit it is offered! Then plan to avoid those behaviours.

Engagement

Assuming you are credible, how to engage then? For the purposes of this book, I am going to sidestep the vast literature on the importance and value to healthcare of physician engagement and how physician engagement may be measured. My focus is on individual leader behaviour to support engagement with one or more people in your orbit, today. David Rock, founder of the Neuroleadership Institute, published the SCARF model for behaviours that will enhance connection and engagement. Rock views engagement from the lens that human social behaviour is governed by a need to minimize threat and maximize reward. Humans have evolved in a state of constant tension between wanting to find and belong in a safe social group and fear of almost everything in a dangerous world around us. We are hardwired for sensitivity to threat or for readiness to run or fight, which can make engagement a challenging task. Rock points out that decisions to engage or disengage with individuals and groups are often made swiftly and subconsciously. These decisions use the same pathways that allow us to instantly evaluate physical threat versus safety in our environment. The SCARF model draws on research that identifies social triggers that inform approach-avoid decisions within the brain. The five elements of SCARF are:

Status: Watch any wildlife documentary about primates and you'll see the importance of status in the group. The association of low status with poorer food, poorer shelter, abuse from higher status members, and greater proximity to predators has been a constant of the last million years or so of human evolution. Settings or behaviour that decrease someone's perception of their status in a situation are likely to be perceived as a threat. This will encourage disengagement. Reassurance or promotion of their status is helpful to engagement efforts.

Certainty: Knowing what to expect, good or bad, is better than not knowing, at least as far as our brains are concerned. Leaders sometimes fall into the trap of tiptoeing around bad news for fear of the backlash it might create, only to make the situation worse by creating uncertainty and associated anxiety.

Autonomy: Just as autonomy is important in our motivation to achieve, it's important in our choices to connect or avoid. When we feel that we have a degree of autonomy over, or even just within, some part of a situation, it creates a sense that we have control over potential stresses or dangers. In my career as a pediatrician, it was often necessary to do an uncomfortable or scary procedure on a child. We would create choices around things like toys on the bed, colour of dressings or tape, who holds their hand, etc., to restore some autonomy in a threat situation. This is just as important for adults, even if the specifics are different.

Relatedness: Like autonomy, this is also important, both in our need to achieve and influencing our decision to connect. We make snap decisions as to whether we are "in" or "out." Being "out" triggers activity in the same regions of the brain responsible for the conscious experience of physical pain. Being "in," on the other hand, is associated with the release of oxytocin, which predisposes us to further likelihood of a positive trust situation.

Fairness: There's a strong possibility that fairness made the list of values you generated in the previous chapter. The concept that we hope to deal with each other with some sense of reciprocity seems to be universal. Primate research suggests it is hard-wired into us. While this trigger may be activated by obviously less than impartial treatment, it's also vulnerable to the type of story-making that occurs when leaders aren't transparent. (We will discuss story-making in a later chapter).

Coach and author Michael Bungay Stanier has adapted Rock's concepts into a simple set of actions that promote engagement with individuals or groups. He has named this the TERA model: Tribe, Expectations, Rank, and Autonomy. Applying this model looks like this:

Tribe: What can I do or say to show we are at least in the same group? This can start with the physical environment. Nothing tells "me" versus "you," or "us" versus "you," like trying to have an important conversation across a big desk, or with parties lined up on either side of a long, imposing table. Are you choosing meeting places that create clear visual boundaries between people? Are you instead choosing spaces that encourage mixing and mingling? What do you and the individuals with whom you want to engage have in common? You may rapidly find professional examples. It's not necessary, however, that the link that joins you be relevant to the issues under consideration. Do you have common outside interests or hobbies, children of similar ages in similar schools, or follow the same sports teams? Did you go to the same university? These are all examples of potential opportunities to create an "in" group connection. Humans have a need for belonging and will subconsciously acknowledge a hit when you find a valid link.

Expectations: Can you identify elements of the issue(s) at hand around which you can create certainty? Can you identify where what is happening now fits into a bigger process and what the likely next steps are?

A good framework for setting expectations can be found from the International Association of Public Participation (IAP2). Their Spectrum of Public Participation, generated to guide the approach to public involvement in policy decisions, translates well to smaller levels and has been adopted by many organizations, including some physician associations and healthcare organizations, to guide interactions between groups. The Spectrum has five parts:

- **Inform** - You are providing objective information and may continue to do so but are not expecting and do not require feedback.

- **Consult** - You are interested in receiving feedback on the information that you have provided. You don't make any commitment to act on what you hear, but you will provide feedback on whether or how the consultation influenced the final decision(s).

- **Involve** - You will work with the individual(s)/group(s) to ensure their ideas are included in the development of alternatives, but you will do the final development and make the final decision.

- **Collaborate** - You will partner with the individual(s)/group(s)/ to develop the alternatives and incorporate their input into final decisions, in which they may have a possibly limited role.

- **Empower** - You place the final decision in their hands and will abide by it.

This simple and elegant framework is not only a good guide for setting expectations for interactions in a professional world but it can also provide insight into where conflict might arise. As written, it suggests that the group on the receiving end is a blank slate whose expectations will be set by the process. But what if that's not true? What if some individual or group is used to occupying a particular place on this spectrum? Physicians in their daily work deal with patients who come to them in search of knowledge and skills to manage their healthcare problems. Day in and day out, physicians are asked to collaborate in complex health matters by their patients. In critical moments, such as in unexpected events in surgery, or in resuscitation and critical care, they're empowered to act without consulting the patient. If someone reaches out to them and isn't explicit about the expectations of the engagement, physicians will tend to assume their usual role: collaborate or empowered. This is often evident in conflict arising around "consultations" with physician groups. Various levels of administration say they consulted physicians, sometimes meaning "Inform," sometimes "Consult," and occasionally "Involve" and "Collaborate." "Empower" is still rare in healthcare system leadership. Physicians often expect "consult" to mean "collaborate" or "empower." They feel devalued and sometimes outraged when that expectation isn't met. They may then become disengaged. Most of these conflicts, and subsequent disengagement, can be avoided if there is an explicit understanding about expectations before the discussion of the topic at hand.

Rank: What can you do or say to eliminate any status gap between you and individual(s) with whom you wish to engage? Are you approaching an encounter dressed in a way that seems to be seeking higher status, such as wearing formal business attire where people tend to dress more casually? Are there contributions the people whom you wish to engage make to you, your role, the organization, or community that need to be acknowledged? Are there special or unique skills or talents they bring to the organization or their patients? Are you able to acknowledge their wisdom or experience that is of value to others in this environment? Is their support or participation critical to success?

Autonomy: What in the situation is an "asteroid," something beyond anyone's control? What is under your control, and what control can you offer to those with whom you seek to engage? Are you able and ready to make clear distinctions between these categories?

Try this exercise. Think about a person or group with whom you need to engage. Write your answers to the following questions:

Tribe:

Are we connecting in a friendly space?

_____

In what group(s) do we all belong?

_____

What interests or characteristics do we have in common?

_____

Expectations:

Why are we engaging (inform, consult, involve, collaborate, empower)?

_____

What can you expect me to do?

_____

What do I expect you to do?

_____

What, if any, are the next steps in our journey together?

_____

Rank:

You are important to me because

_____

I can shrink any status gap between us by

_____

You are important in what is happening here because

_____

I/we value you/your input/help because

_____

Autonomy:

These things are beyond our control:

_____

You are free to choose in the following areas:

_____

Did you notice that none of these questions get into the meat of a specific issue? Often, meetings move directly to substance without any attention paid to what needs to be done to secure engagement. Such meetings often fail to achieve their objectives. Indeed, one of the most common mistakes in engagement is thinking that having a meeting and people showing up is evidence engagement has happened. If you want a meaningful dialogue, particularly in sensitive or delicate matters, work on engagement first and substance later. View meetings as opportunities to create engagement, not as examples of engagement.

In response to frequent "just in time" requests for support in this area, I have developed an even simpler arrangement of the drivers of engagement, the 3 Cs approach. This uses similar elements to TERA but emphasizes the leader's actions, rather than the content. The Cs are:

- **Connect** anyway you can. Find whatever possibilities exist to create an in-group connection.

- **Certify** your status, my status and what is happening here. Reduce anxiety in the relationship by establishing as much certainty as possible about roles and expectations.

- **Cede** control wherever possible. Be proactive about finding ways to share or create autonomy.

Meanwhile, Sanjay and Christine are continuing their conversation …

"Tell me, Sanjay, how many members of your department can you name on sight?"

"Well, all of them, of course!"

"In my experience, you can never assume 'of course.' But good for you; that's a good start. With how many of them have you ever had a non-patient-related conversation lasting more than ten minutes?"

Sanjay thought for a second. "I don't know—maybe ten."

"So, when it comes to some sort of personal connection, you're already down to less than half your department. Not unusual in this day and age. How many partners or families have you met?"

"Maybe five or six."

"If I asked your department members questions about you as a person, not as a medical specialist, how many would be able to give answers?"

"Again, maybe five or six."

"How do you feel when someone you don't know and who has never shown interest in you summons you to a meeting."

"That's a bit harsh, but I guess I'd say that depends on the meeting topic."

"That's exactly right. You want them to engage, but you're hanging your whole enterprise on them making a cool, rational decision about the subject material rather than on who is calling the meeting. In my experience, cool, rational decisions are a rare commodity, particularly for busy, stressed people. On the other hand, how do you feel if someone with whom you feel a connection asks to join in something?"

"I probably would go, unless there was a good reason not to."

"So, if there's no connection, your default position is no to maybe, unless there's a good reason to engage. If there is a connection, your default position is yes, unless there's a good reason not to. Let's put the idea of making personal connections with your department members on the table as a possible change to your approach. But let's just park that for now, because there are some other points I don't want to lose. What did you want to get from that meeting?"

"I wanted to float some ideas for the department and see what people thought."

"You wanted their input to a vision for the department?"

"Yes, that's right"

"Was that obvious in the invite?"

Sanjay was quiet for a moment. "Actually, when you put it like that, I sent out my ideas as a bit of a manifesto; I didn't explicitly ask for feedback."

"What were the department members expecting from that meeting?"

"I don't know—I didn't really think about it."

"You sent out a notice about your view of the world, and you didn't ask theirs. What message does that send?"

Sanjay winced. "That I don't care what they think?"

Christine nodded. "Something like that. At least that they weren't foremost in your thinking. Let me propose that having choices is very important to people. In the situation we've just described, what was the one clear choice you gave to your department members?"

Sanjay thought for a second. "The only one really was ... do I come to the meeting or not?"

Christine smiled. "Exactly!"

Sanjay shook his head. "I've really screwed this up, haven't I?"

"I wouldn't say it was the strongest start I've ever seen, but it's far from the worst, and with a bit of work, you can get this back on track. Think back on what we just covered, and now tell me how you'll re-do it."

"Well, I guess I need to take the time to meet the department members."

"Good; tell me how."

"I could start booking one-on-one or one-on-two coffee breaks, and maybe try to meet two to four of them a week for the next two or three months."

"Great idea. What are you going to talk about?"

"I guess the best thing would be whatever they want to talk about. Anything is likely to put me further ahead in understanding them than where I am now."

"Really good. What aren't you going to talk about?"

Sanjay thought for a second. "Wasn't expecting that question. I guess I should be careful talking about me and my agenda until I understand where they're coming from."

"Something like that. It's fair to comment or inform people on stuff you know is falling out of the sky that's beyond your control, provided you're careful to be listening to those bits where their opinions are going to matter. So, who's first?"

"I ... I don't know."

"I would suggest Gwen."

"Talk about starting at the deep end. She's already opposing me!"

"Is she? I heard you say that she challenged you to justify what you were doing, and that she pointed to a weakness in your approach, but she did show up. Did you know that she holds the record for the growth of the number of specialists and programs during the tenure of a department head? She may be a bit caustic at times, but she's very passionate about your department and this hospital."

"You think I can get her on side?"

"I think she might be open to it, or she wouldn't have come to the meeting."

Sanjay smiled. "Thanks, I feel a lot better. I'll start on this stuff today."

"Sooner the better. How about the next time you call a special department meeting, give me a call first and let's just brainstorm a bit how you present it."

Key Learnings

- *Leadership requires the ability to engage and inspire followers.*

- *Engage followers using the tenets of the SCARF model; establish Status, create Certainty, offer Autonomy, support Relatedness, and demonstrate Fairness.*

- *Practice engagement in all your encounters by finding ingroup connections, creating certainty around status and expectations, and surrendering control wherever possible.*

- *Be a credible leader; emphasize the future, your followers, and their contributions, act fearlessly, communicate well, and be the most willing to learn new things and accept constructive criticism.*

- *Be a trustworthy leader; do as you say you will do, protect the group, live your and the organization's values, listen to stakeholders, acknowledge the success of others.*

FURTHER READING

Followership

Robert E. Kelley, "In Praise of Followers," *Harvard Business Review,* 66, Issue 6 (1988): 142–148.

Robert E. Kelley, *The Power of Followership: How to Create Leaders People Want to Follow and Followers Who Lead Themselves* (New York NY: Doubleday. 1992).

Barbara Kellerman, "What Every Leader Needs to Know about Followers," *Harvard Business Review,* 85, December (2007:84–91).

Barbara Kellerman, *Followership: How Followers Are Creating Change and Changing Leaders* (Boston, Mass: Harvard Business School Press, 2008).

David A. Watters, Kyleigh Smith, Stephen Tobin, and Spencer W. Beasley, "Follow the Leader: Followership and Its Relevance for Surgeons," *ANZ J Surg,* Volume 89 (2019): 589–593.

Credibility

Daniel Han Ming Chng, Tae-Yeol Kim, Brad Gilbreath, and Lynne Andersson, "Why People Believe in Their Leaders—or Not," *MIT Sloan Management Review,* 60, Fall (2018), 65–70.

Lara Hazelton and Michelle MacDonald, "Building Belief: Establishing Credibility as a Medical Leader," *Canadian Journal of Physician Leadership,* 7(2021): 100–107.

Engagement

David Rock, "SCARF: A Brain-Based Model for Collaborating with and Influencing Others," *Neuroscience Journal,* 1(2008): 44–53.

Michael Bungay Stanier, "Three Habits to Have Your People with You not Against You," August 1, 2021, https://boxofcrayons.com/2015/07/three-habits-to-have-your-people-with-you-not-against-you/.

International Association of Public Participation, "IAP2 Spectrum of Public Participation," August 1, 2021, https://www.iap2.org/page/pillars.

DIDN'T THEY TELL YOU THAT YOU'RE CHAIRING THE MEETING?

Rosalind comes through the administration office area on her way to her office. Anita, the administrative assistant she shares with the hospital administrator, calls her over.

"The Medical Advisory Committee is next Wednesday. I should send out the agenda today. Do you have anything for it?"

Rosalind's shoulders slump. She's been putting off dealing with the MAC in the busy first few days in her role, so much so that it managed to sneak up on her. She attended these meetings in her previous capacity as Department Head for Emergency. Each meeting consists of "rubber stamping" the latest batch of medical staff privilege requests and hearing occasional updates or announcements from the hospital administrator and verbal, often disorganized, department reports. Many of these are just venting on the same topic month after month. Sometimes, guests from various services within the region come to present, but the hostile atmosphere that's brewed by the monthly vent often means that they're treated less than respectfully.

"Just put me down for an introduction before the departmental round table."

Anita nods. "Okay. I have the minutes from the last meeting and the privileges package that I'll send out with the agenda." She pauses. "Can I ask you something?"

"Sure," replies Rosalind.

"Don't take this the wrong way. I mean, everyone on that committee is a great doc and works really hard, I know... but that's the most difficult meeting to take minutes for, particularly as I have to stay back late to be there. I was wondering if we could find some time to talk about that. Not now, I know you're just finding your way around, but soon."

Rosalind had been embarrassed for Anita in the past for some of the comments and exchanges she was forced to witness in that meeting. She can't begin to imagine what it must be like to untangle the random comments and people talking over each other to produce succinct minutes, which Anita does really well. She has an anxious moment worrying that Anita might be trying to get out of the role—not that she would blame her.

"Certainly. I've had some concerns myself. I'd appreciate any ideas on how we can make the meeting work better, particularly if it makes it easier for you."

Later that day, Rosalind has a check-in call with Jim, the regional Executive Medical Director, who calls or sits in on the MAC meetings three or four times per year. She expresses her frustrations with the meeting, and her anxiety that it may be impacting the support staff.

Jim is thoughtful for a moment. "What's that saying about 'what you walk by'?"

Rosalind replies. "The standard you walk by is the standard you accept. It was originally made famous in the context of violence against women, but it's been appropriated in a lot of other contexts."

"No disrespect to its original use, but it does rather capture this issue, don't you think? If I asked everyone else who comes to that meeting, including Anita, how they experience it, do you think I would hear anything different?"

Rosalind reflects on faces and body language of past meetings, particularly as people get up to leave. She struggles to find anything that suggests people were enjoying themselves.

"Probably not."

"Well, the meeting is mandated by the Medical Staff Bylaws, but the sort of experience it becomes is up to the people who attend. You're the Chair, so it's your meeting now. Tell me what this meeting will look like if you choose to stop walking by the usual way it runs."

Planning the Meeting

Meetings seem to be the bane of physician leaders' existence. Yet if there were no meetings, how would physician leaders demonstrate and implement their leadership? Can we imagine a world where physician leaders lead as disembodied voices or floating holograms of a cowled head, giving orders like the Emperor in *Star Wars*? Do we want to? Meetings are truly where leadership rubber hits the road. Think of a leader with whom you have worked, whom you respected and admired. Think of the meetings they ran. While there's not a perfect correlation, you probably are more likely to reflect more favourably on their meetings than less respected leaders in your journey. Good meeting skills are invaluable for good leaders. The word "skills" is used here very deliberately. Good meetings are not ensured by an encyclopedic knowledge of Robert's Rules of Order. They are a set of learned abilities that do the following:

- get the right people to a meeting

- provide clarity on the meeting's purpose

- support meaningful, respectful, and insightful discussion

- have a clear paradigm for making decisions

- establish clear expectations of action and accountability for those actions

- generate a clear, easily accessible, and accurate record of proceedings

- achieve all of this in the minimum amount of time required to assure good process.

To explore some options on making your meetings more productive, this chapter will walk though the process of a typical meeting, from the decision to hold a meeting through to follow up after the meeting. The process will presume that the meeting involves several people who have some shared purpose. Conducting one-on-one meetings will be covered in more detail in the chapter on significant conversations, although many of the same principles apply.

I don't propose to do a detailed breakdown of every possible type of meeting here. If you're interested in templates for different levels of meetings, Cameron Herald's book *Meetings Suck* is a good resource. Physician leaders may lead anything from five-minute daily huddles on clinical units to meetings of large organizational boards of directors. Perhaps surprisingly, the principles for getting value for time invested are similar at both ends of this spectrum.

Do You Need a Meeting?

Meetings can be addictive. They spread in calendars like some form fungus or corrosion. Think of a meeting that you're planning to arrange and answer these two questions:

What purpose am I hoping to achieve?

_____

Specifically, how will this meeting make this happen?

_____

If you have a clear answer to both questions, you have a purpose for a meeting. If not, you need to reconsider.

Putting aside meetings that are required to happen for some legislated or regulatory purpose, let's look at some examples:

> *Example 1. A new policy has been brought in at your hospital/ clinic. Its effects are minor, but you need people to be aware of it. There's no option to adjust or amend it. The people responsible for writing the policy will not be available to discuss it.*

This would best be circulated as a document for information.

Example 2. A new building is being planned, and the consultants involved in functional planning need input from physicians on workflow. There has been no prior consultation.

The first part of the process described above is interrogation, to gather information. If you're planning a properly facilitated focus group, go for it. Bringing together a group of busy people without preparation to gather specific technical information is a bad idea. Consider using succinct questionnaires or push the consultants to approach people individually.

Example 3. A group of managers/leaders at a similar level in the organization meet monthly, as the CEO thought it would be a good idea. The group does not have a specific mandate and doesn't report to or advise anyone in the executive structure.

This type of meeting is surprisingly common; I call them "Leaders Anonymous" groups. The problem is that unlike the group from which I drew the name, they lack a clear approach and don't have a clear purpose to serve the membership that attends. These can either be a complete waste of time or a great opportunity. If someone(s) steps up and defines a purpose that provides benefit to those that attend, they can be invaluable for peer support and organizational learning. If they're left to drift, they tend to fester into time wasted in whining and complaint.

Example 4. A decision is pending on a choice of introducing new services to a hospital and possibly moving others to a nearby ambulatory clinic. The decision is not final, and the Executive want some sense of how members of the medical staff feel. The alternatives are publicly available.

Here there is a purpose—the gathering of information, including (importantly) feelings. This is different from the workflow example above, which is focused on more objective details. While surveys could be used here, meetings are better for assessing the emotional temperature. This can call for skill in managing those emotions, but good planning and good leadership take emotional issues into account.

Who Do I Need at the Meeting?

The word "need" is deliberate. Try to limit meeting invitations to those without whom the purpose cannot be achieved. Careless direction of meeting invitations to a large cast is a good way to annoy people. When you ask physicians to come to a meeting, you're asking them to donate their most precious resource: time. For everyone on the list, you need to be able to answer:

Why does this person need to attend the meeting?

_____

Do they need to attend for the whole meeting, or can they come in just for a specific time?

_____

Does the Meeting Invite Make People Want to Attend?

The meeting invitation is where your meeting really starts. Visualize this situation. You open your email and sitting there is a meeting request. The request comes from a person you don't know. The meeting title is an acronym that you don't recognize, and you've already booked the time of the meeting for something upon which you place high value. There's no accompanying information. Now become aware of your bodily sensations. Did your jaw clench a bit? Did you feel something not quite pleasant in your gut? Did your eyes narrow? Were you aware of your heart and breathing rates accelerating slightly? The chances are good that you experienced some or all the above. What your body is telling you is that it saw the meeting invitation as a threat. Having once registered it as a threat, your brain will make that the default setting for anything associated with that meeting going forward. Can you imagine what that sort of subconscious programming is going to do to the probability that someone will come to the meeting? If they do attend, can you imagine the frame of mind they'll likely bring with them?

Now think back on what you learned about engagement in the last chapter. Imagine a meeting invitation that clearly identifies the group being called together to meet (Tribe/group). It specifies the reason for the meeting and what is hoped to come out of it (Expectations). It includes a personal note as to why the organizer feels it's important that you specifically join (Rank/Status). It offers an alternate time or an alternate mechanism for contributing to the issue (Autonomy/Choice). This type of meeting request recognizes that demands on the time of busy people are inherently threatening, and it works hard to defuse that threat. Try it out! You can set up a template for your meeting invites that looks something like this:

> "*Dear <insert name here>,*
>
> *I am calling a meeting of <insert group name here—avoid acronyms if possible> in order to <action verb here> <subject of meeting here>. It is important because <reason for importance>. We need to accomplish this by <time frame> because <reason for time frame>. I would really value your presence because <individual contribution of recipient>. If this time doesn't work, I am holding < alternate time> as an alternate. If neither work, let me know and I will send you the relevant materials and invite your written feedback, which I will introduce to the meeting."*

Do You Have an Agenda?

An agenda is perhaps the most important meeting tool there is. It is, or rather it should be, much more than a list of topics to be discussed. A good agenda is the roadmap of the meeting. It establishes what is in bounds and what is out of bounds. There are many ways to write agendas; it's a matter of personal choice and style. Whatever layout is preferred, effective agendas tend to contain several common elements for each item:

- **Topic** - A clear descriptive title of what is being discussed. Avoid acronyms, as they often mean different things for people from different backgrounds. This is a common cause of confusion and sometimes embarrassment.

- **Presenter** - Assign topics to the person best suited to lead the discussion. This helps support participation and is a good way of fairly distributing responsibility for the success of the meeting.

- **Time allocated** - This is imperative. It creates incentive to keep the meeting on track and discussion relevant. Having to make a realistic allocation of time to a topic helps prevent "stuffing" the meeting so that some items are lost when time runs out.

- **Details/background** - A succinct summary of the issue and supporting documentation.

- **Expected outcome** - This is also very important. For each request to add to a meeting agenda, require the person requesting to commit to an outcome. Is it for information only? Is it for discussion and consultation? Is a decision required? If so, can the decision be framed as a yes/no question, or a motion to be included in the agenda? Is it being prepared for referral to another group? If items are coming for information only, be very stingy about assigning valuable meeting time to them. If regulatory requirements demand that certain reports are included and accepted, consider using a consent agenda item where all of these are grouped together under a single motion, unless someone at the meeting asks for a specific item to be brought out for more detailed examination.

The running of a meeting can be helped by allowing time on the agenda for a few other things:

- Items carried over or requiring follow up from a previous meeting. This is often included as "Business Arising" after approval of the minutes of a previous meeting, if your process is that formal. A common failing, however, is to not treat business arising items with the same precision as new agenda items. These too should have someone clearly identified as accountable for them, an action expectation, and a time limit. Failure to do this can derail your meeting almost before it has started.

- A parking lot. This is where you put things that come up during discussion that may be important but are not germane when they arise.

Put a few minutes into the agenda at the end of the meeting to deal with these. Decide whether they no longer need to be discussed, whether they can be sorted quickly now, if they should be put on the agenda of a future meeting, or whether they should be referred to another setting (delete, discuss, defer, or delegate). If either of the latter two options are chosen, create clear accountability as to who will perform those actions and when they will occur.

- Meeting summary. Use this time at the end of the meeting to review decisions and actions and confirm assignment of accountability. Invite comments and suggestions about how the running of the meeting can be improved.

An example of an agenda that captures these principles can be seen in Figure 3.

Figure 3.

St. Somewhere Regional Community Hospital Medical Advisory Committee Meeting May21, 2021, 1700–1830 Hours
Agenda

Item	Speaker	Time (minutes)	Detail	Action required
1. Approve Agenda	Chair	2	Approve agenda, including additions or deletions	Decision
2. Minutes- Previous meeting	Chair	2	Approve minutes April 16th meeting	Decision
3. Business arising: 3.1. Urgent CT requests	Dr. J. Alvarez Dept. Head DI	5	Endorse amended out of hours CT protocol (attached)	Decision
3.2. Ambulatory Clinic build	Ms. E. Jones Hospital Administrator	10	Revise information on completion timelines and move in sequence	Discussion
4. Consent Agenda	Chair	5	Receive regular reports and accept as required by bylaws (attached)	Decision

Item	Speaker	Time (minutes)	Detail	Action required
5. Privileges and Credentials	Dr. A. Ahmed Chair, Credentials Committee	10	Review and approve privilege and credential requests and renewals (full package attached)	Decision
6. Recruitment	Dr. M. Gbeho Chair, Recruitment Committee	5	Update on recruitments in progress (spread-sheet attached)	Information
7. New Business: 7.1 Staff Appreciation events	Ms. E. Jones, Hospital Administrator	5	Review planned events and seek physician participation	Information
7.2 Changes to Troponin assays	Dr. J. Agarwal, Dept. Head Clin. Chem.	5	Review and approve changes in reference range re: time from cardiac event and changes in protocols (attached)	Decision
7.3 Departmental responsibility for physician vaca-tion coverage	Chair	15	Review correspondence on concerns about short-notice physician vacations and adverse impact on continuity of care (attached). Explore creation of working group to develop clearer policy	Discussion / Decision
8. Parking lot	Chair	5		Discussion/ Decision
9. Round table	All	15	Any significant issues or cel-ebrations from departments	Information
10. Meeting summary	Chair	5	Review decisions and confirm assignment of next steps	Information
11. Adjourn				

An example of a well-structured formal agenda

Running the Meeting

Do You Have Agreements about Process and Behaviour?

Have you ever been in a meeting where discussion just kept swirling and issues got lost in "how are we supposed to do this" discussions? Such meetings are the outcome when there's no time spent establishing a process, or ground rules, if you prefer, for the meeting. If your meeting is a spontaneous one, or an ad hoc group pulled together quickly for a specific purpose, a discussion at the beginning of the meeting and some jotted notes on a pad or flip chart will suffice. If your meeting is with a more formal group with some official standing, it should have written Terms of Reference. This can be a good place to include these policies.

There are few simple ground rules that will help any meeting:

- **We start on time** - This one should seem self evident, but the loss of five or ten minutes at the beginning of meetings, waiting for a previous meeting to clear a room, waiting for laggards, or struggling with technology is common. Where set up is required, allow a few minutes before the meeting to ensure you're ready

- **Technology policy** - It's unrealistic in this age of instant availability to expect physicians or other professionals to leave their phones outside the meeting, with rare exceptions. It is realistic to ask people to put phones on vibrate and step outside, or in a virtual meeting, mute sound and cancel their video feed while they take the call. The phone conversation represents a novel stimulus. It takes truly superhuman concentration on the part of others in the room to shut it out and focus on the business at hand. The Chair must be firm and polite about enforcing this.

- **Speaker recognition and order** - It's excellent practice at the start of every meeting to remind everyone what your process is for being recognized to speak, and to ask that people wait their turn. It's also good practice to ask that people only speak when they wish to add something that hasn't already been said. A good chair will be capturing the important elements of the discussion and be ready to summarize before a decision.

- **Be clear on how you make decisions** - Don't wait until you have a life and death issue in front of you to decide whether you hold votes or not. If your group is a decision-making body, you should have a clear policy on how you make decisions. If you go with voting, have a clear process for calling a vote. You should also have a process for breaking ties. If you decide that your group will work on a basis of obtaining consensus, you need definitions of what consensus means. Does it mean everyone likes the idea? Does it mean most like it and others can live with it? You must also have a process for when consensus can't be obtained. In groups that are advisory, this can often be easily handled by issuing majority and minority reports. In groups that must act, it can become more complicated. Options include offline discussions with individuals, referral to a higher authority, or some form of arbitration or other agreed dispute-resolution mechanism. A full discussion of consensus frameworks is beyond the scope of this book. Where there is a lot at stake, consultation with an expert in governance matters can be very helpful.

- **Have a system to record the meeting and an agreed-upon location where records can be found** - This will be covered in more detail later in this chapter. For most purposes, if the record isn't comprehensible or can't be found, the meeting might as well have not happened.

- **Have an agreed ending time** - In the section on agenda, I emphasized the importance of summarizing the meeting, confirming decisions, and assigning accountabilities. In order to slot that in, you must know the meeting end time in advance. If you run the discussion right up until the moment people are walking out the door or hitting the "leave meeting" button online, you won't know if critical messages were received or not.

Do You Have Your Meeting Team in Place?

The hardest part of chairing a meeting is listening to and capturing the essence of the discussion. For the meeting to run well, someone must be keeping their eyes open for speaking requests and maintaining a list of speakers in the order of requests. Someone must be keeping track of time and giving notice when it's running short. Someone needs to be keeping minutes. Assigning one person to do everything a good meeting requires risks nothing being done well. Chairing a meeting is a great example of leadership being accountable that things get done while not doing everything yourself. Even if the meeting is down to two people, agree who is taking notes. With a larger group, assigning different people to manage the speaker list, keep time, and keep minutes frees the Chair to focus on the discussion, guide the decision-making process, and manage meeting behaviour—more than enough for a full-time job. There's an additional benefit to sharing the load, particularly in tense meetings. By asking individuals to take a role in running the meeting, you are conferring status and autonomy, which will support their engagement with the process. Consider offering these roles not only to your supporters but also to those who might oppose what is being discussed. Offering trust is a good way to receive it.

Do You Have a System for Recording the Meeting?

This is likely not a huge issue for formal organizational meetings. Most large healthcare organizations have some standard policy and often prepared templates for meeting minutes. Skill is still required by the Chair to summarize and support the drafting of motions and decisions. Skill is also required in capturing the information, although modern recording technology and laptop computers have certainly assisted. For smaller, less formal meetings not supported by someone solely dedicated to transcription, this can be very challenging. My physician coaching colleague, Mary T. Yates of Align Associates, has developed a simple system to support physician leaders in this situation, called the 3 As: Agreement, Actions from the Agreement, Accountability. These can be combined in a template, an example of which is found in Figure 4. When an agreement seems to be reached, the chair should articulate exactly what has been agreed upon. Using a flip chart, a white board, or a virtual white board to write it down and track amendments before polling for agreement is very helpful. Having secured the agreement, it's prudent to confirm the actions and accountabilities before moving on. Take some time at the end to review the whole set of agreements and actions. Be aware of potential imbalances in the burden of work and responsibility, and be explicit in asking for how people feel about the fairness of what has been done, for example, "I notice Elaine has a few more things on her list now than anyone else. Can we look at that again?" Confirm the accountability and the timeline with the individual(s) concerned before finally recording it.

Figure 4.

3A Minutes			
Agreements	**Actions arising from Agreements**	**Accountability**	
Agreement 1	Actions	Who	When
Agreement 2	Actions	Who	When
Agreement 3	Actions	Who	When

3As System for Recording a Meeting. © Mary T. Yates, 2016 (reproduced with permission)

After the Meeting

Having successfully completed your meeting, your work is not done. As soon as possible, and preferably within forty-eight hours while memories are still fresh, send out draft minutes or a summary and invite corrections. Include in that message a thank you for participating in the meeting. These sorts of simple acknowledgements have a significant effect in the neurophysiology and psychology that influence the perceptions people will build of working in that group. If someone's contribution stood out, acknowledge it individually. If there are individual accountabilities for specific tasks arising out of the meeting, send short individual messages thanking those people for taking these on, and summarize the specifics of the tasks. Set aside a specific time in your calendar to do this for all non-casual meetings. A commitment of fifteen minutes may save you hours of frustration.

Before the Next Meeting

If your meeting is a recurring one, set aside some time in your calendar a few days beforehand to prepare. Other than any material you may need to present, as Chair of the meeting, you need to cover the following tasks:

- **Send out the meeting invitation or reminder** - Take a few minutes to make the invitation inviting, as discussed earlier in this chapter.

- **Check in with those with accountabilities from the previous meeting** - This could be a polite email reminder, but if the person's actions/input are critical, you may want to consider giving them a call. Offer support or a pre-meeting if needed. Reschedule their piece to another meeting if they cannot be prepared. This avoids wasted time for other participants and potential embarrassment to those who have been unable to meet their original intended deadlines for whatever reason.

- **Ask for an RSVP if a critical mass of participants is required**
  - Be prepared to reschedule if participation is insufficient for the purpose.

Virtual Meetings

This book was written at the height of the COVID-19 pandemic in 2021, when almost all meetings were virtual. While the pandemic dramatically increased the number of such meetings, they were common before the pandemic. For some organizations, including healthcare organizations managing multiple programs in large geographic areas, they were already the norm (those or blended in-person and virtual meetings).

Good meeting practice for virtual meetings includes all the good practices for in-person meetings, but they do have some additional nuances.

- **Be sure of your technology** - While you can't protect against all calamities, be sure your technology works. For larger groups, where monitoring chat rooms or managing virtual breakout rooms are involved, don't try to do it alone. Get dedicated help to manage the technology. Have a phone number people can call if they're having issues.

- **Make time for the personal** - Research before the pandemic identified a greater risk of feeling isolated amongst remote workers. In an earlier chapter, I emphasized the importance of feeling connected to a group as part of engagement. Even the small amounts of social interaction that occur waiting outside a meeting room or exchanging pleasantries after an in-person meeting count. Where virtual has become the only contact, adding the few minutes at the beginning of the meeting to check in with everyone is a human touch. Such check-ins work better if they're specific. Asking "How are you doing?" risks getting a chorus of "Fine," with no one wishing to seem the weak link.

Emerging research in the US reveals that people moved to remote working by the pandemic were most stressed about family, children, school, and home friction generated by multiple workplaces and school demanding technology and bandwidth. These loomed larger than concerns about job security or personal health risk. When you do a check in, ask about real issues. For example, "I'd like to hear how everybody is handling working from home and if there's anything that can be done to help." At the end of the meeting, leaving the meeting room open for fifteen minutes after adjournment for anyone who wants some group chat time is often appreciated. This is easy to do with personal Zoom accounts but may require formal booking on organizational systems.

- **Track the participation** - A good chair notices who is talking and who is not in any meeting, and virtual meetings are no exception. Working through video may make the more introverted even less willing to speak up, so checking in with the quiet ones and getting yea or nay one at a time on important questions are good practices. Do not assume silence is consent.

- **Discourage multitasking** - Video makes this harder to do than with teleconferences but watch for the signs that someone is disconnected. Look for a non-threatening way to bring them back into the conversation. Not only are they not fully engaged in your meeting but there's also evidence that this sort of behaviour increases limbic system activity in a similar way to physical and psychological threat. This results in reduced prefrontal cortex activity in the brain, reducing higher cognitive functions.

- **Recognize that videoconferencing may be harder work** - Objective measured proof of this is probably yet to exist. Having made that disclaimer, the number of reports of personal experience of "Zoom fatigue" is huge and includes some very astute thinkers. Professor Jeremy Bailenson at Stanford has raised fascinating arguments firmly based in prior psychological research as to why we should expect problems. Potential stressors include an abnormal amount of close-distance eye gaze, increased effort with sending and receiving non-verbal cues, the impact of seeing oneself on screen for extended periods, and dramatically reduced mobility compared to other meeting scenarios. While experimental proof is still pending, the arguments are persuasive. In some ways, the boom in videoconferencing has a potentially negative effect on our first meeting condition in this chapter—only hold the meetings you need. Personal computer-based videoconferencing technology has freed us from room-bookings and travel-time considerations. I have software that sets these meetings up at a single mouse click by a client. But as soon as I have three hours booked in a day, I close bookings; I know from experience that is my limit. We have a great responsibility to ensure we're not just calling a videoconference as a lazy option for our own benefit. No one yet knows how much videoconference time is too much. Until we do, we should give people space to say that they really are unable to handle another videoconference that day.

Handling Poor Meeting Behaviour

The complaints about meetings that come in coaching sessions tend to fall into one of two categories. The first is that certain meetings are a waste of time because they fail to achieve anything. The second, which may overlap with the first, is a dread of the behaviour that will be on display at the meeting. This is a significant cause of stress for physician leaders. They often perceive that their ability to sanction or control the behaviour of other physicians is much more limited than for more standard employer-employee relationships.

Research conducted within the Amazon organization has emphasized what it at stake with controlling poor meeting behaviour. Nale Lehman-Willenbrok, Joseph Allen, and Dain Belyeu used sophisticated survey and statistical techniques to explore the influence of good and bad meeting behaviours. They found that counterproductive meeting behaviour was the strongest single influence on employee satisfaction, but also on emotional exhaustion and engagement. No single positive behaviour had an equivalent effect to counter this negative one.

Poor meeting behaviour tends to follow certain common patterns and may warrant specific types of responses. Before I go into these, there are some things you can do that will generally reduce the risk of a disrupted meeting. These include:

- **Engagement, engagement, engagement** - Reinforce group connections, expectations, status, and autonomy at every opportunity. Antony Jay, in his 1976 *Harvard Business Review* article, considered one of the best references in existence for running meetings laid out the functions of a meeting with the engagement components listed in just those terms. People who want to be at a meeting are also more likely to want it to succeed. Watch for "us vs. them" thinking and move in quickly to create "we're all in this together" concepts. Remember, just calling a meeting is not engaging with people; it just creates an opportunity for engagement.

- **Good meeting rules** - Rules on speaker order and non-repetition can have a huge impact on meeting conduct. They need to be politely and consistently enforced. Most people will respond to such measures.

- **Acknowledge and manage emotion in the room** - Generally, if you want to create an explosion, you first need to confine a volatile reaction, which given open air instead, may burn itself out harmlessly. If someone looks upset or angry, don't be afraid to surface it and address it. There's evidence from the emotional-intelligence realm that naming the emotion in aroused states can reduce detrimental limbic system activity and support higher cognitive functions. Acknowledging emotion in risky situations has been empirically shown to enhance trust. Trying something like "John, I'm getting the sense that you have concerns about what we're saying. I'd like to hear about how you're experiencing this before we go any further." It may feel like you're opening up yourself and your meeting to an assault. What follows such invitations, however, particularly if guided with a few skillful questions, is usually much less explosive than if negative emotion is allowed to build without an outlet. How to handle such conversations is covered in more detail in a later chapter.

- **Don't push past people's limits** - Meetings that are too long, too late in the day, or that involve hungry, thirsty, or tired people are asking for trouble.

- **Share responsibility for running the meeting** - Particularly where you may have some sort of factions forming, share accountability for meeting functions as widely as you can.

- **Don't be afraid to pull the plug** - If the meeting is truly out of control, point out that no progress is being made, adjourn, and reconvene after some individual consultations and damage control. You'll get some criticism for doing that, but also some thanks from those not enjoying the spectacle.

Accepting that everyone has bad days and deserves some consideration, there are certain patterns of recurring behaviour that commonly disrupt meetings. Managing some of these behaviours in front of other meeting participants is often uncomfortable for the Chair and those watching. It's helpful to acknowledge these feelings after the efforts at managing the behaviours have concluded. When confronting these behaviours, be careful to identify the behaviour, identify the impact of the behaviour, identify the alternate, desired behaviour, and invite compliance. It needs to be about the behaviour, not the person. Be careful not to confront, antagonize, or accuse.

Common counterproductive meeting behaviours include:

- **The Laggard** - This individual is always late. In the meeting, don't wait for them. If they were due to present, reschedule to another time, and don't reshuffle the meeting to accommodate them. After the meeting, arrange a short one-on-one to explain the impact of their behaviour and invite them to propose solutions. An example of the language of such a conversation might be, "I notice that, while our meetings are scheduled to start at 3:00 p.m., you've arrived around 3:15 at the last three meetings. I'm concerned that you're missing important parts of the discussion and breaking the flow of the conversation. I really need you to be available when the meeting is due to start, or if that's not possible, help me find an alternate who can cover your role. What do we need to accomplish that?" If the behaviour persists, consider escalation in the appropriate direction to have them replaced in the group.

- **The Bore** - This person keeps bringing up the same point again and again, often meeting after meeting. They often fail to respect speaking order. It's certainly fair to control it in the meeting with fair application of the non-repetition rule. Use language like "I notice that you've made that exact point several times already. Our time is limited, and time spent recovering ground is potentially time lost to explore other possibilities. I'd like to ask that you only take the floor if you have something new to add." Repeated failure to respect the speaking order rule can precipitate a request that they leave the meeting, or a suggestion to adjourn, as they are preventing progress. If that proves inadequate, it's time for a one-on-one conversation. It's worth considering whether the perseveration on a specific point is a sign of an emotionally triggered state caused by perception of threat. When we're in such a state, we only register incoming information that aligns with our mental model of what's happening. We're also prone to being hijacked by memory or past perceptions rather than what's happening around us. This type of conversation is a bit deep for most group venues and is best raised in a separate one-on-one.

- **The Angry Beast** - This individual always comes in spoiling for a fight. They may be prone to outbursts while not respecting the agreed speaking order. As with the example above, repeated failure to respect the speaking order rule can precipitate a request that they leave the meeting, or a suggestion to adjourn, as they are preventing progress. There's a well described physiological phenomenon called "emotional contagion" in which our social programming allows the emotional state of others to become reproduced in our own psyches. Angry beasts can sow emotional discord around a meeting. Try something like "I can see you feel very strongly about this. I'd like to give you an opportunity to help us understand why this is upsetting for you, but I must insist that you keep your tone and language respectful and appropriate. Upsetting others will not help them hear what you want to say. I'm happy to hear how you're experiencing this, but I cannot permit you to make assertions or accusations about your colleagues." If surfacing the anger doesn't work, you may have to consider escalation to either encouraging this person to better manage these issues or replacing them in your group. It is, however, critical to do something. If you don't confront this pattern of behaviour, the angry beast will eventually take your group hostage against triggering their anger.

- **The Martyr** - This person is most commonly complaining about work/psychological stress. Sometimes, it will be someone who goes to great pains to make sure everyone in the room is aware that they are there at the cost of great personal physical discomfort. The trick here is not to be "fused" and feel responsible for their experience. They've a made a choice to be there. In the meeting, a good response is to be empathetic but emphasize the choice: "I'm sorry to hear you're feeling that way. If you find yourself in too much discomfort, feel free to leave, and we'll fill you in later." Outside the meeting, be prepared to have a frank conversation with them and their superiors as to whether they are up to the role.

- **The Commentator** - This individual is always making sotto voce comments and trying to draw others into side conversations. Don't tolerate it. Start with general comments: "Please, can we just have one person speaking at a time? It's very difficult to hear clearly when there are other conversations going on." Then move to the specific: "Judy, if you have something to add to this, could you please add your name to the speaker list and share it with all of us?" If the behaviour persists, have an explicit one-on-one conversation outside of the meeting and consider escalation or replacement.

Let's see how Rosalind got on ...

Rosalind comes in the door at home at about 8:00 p.m.

"You're late," says Susan. "I thought your meeting was going to finish at 6.30."

"Well, that meeting did, but a lot of stuff happened, and a few folks asked to stay back and chat."

"So, what happened?"

"After talking to Jim, he gave me a few names of people he thought were really good at running meetings, and I made a few calls and got a few ideas. The first thing I did today was put up a flip chart and introduce three meeting rules: everybody speaks in turn; everyone only speaks when they have something new to add; and we stick to time. A couple of people had a real problem with the first rule, but by the end of the meeting, other people were calling them on it. It was great. I then used my time on the agenda to ask people how we could make this meeting work better for them. We got some good ideas, and a few people stepped up to form a working group to get this moving—that was what went on overtime."

"So, all the tossing and turning last night was for nothing."

Rosalind smiles sheepishly. "I guess so. I'm excited to see how this new MAC redesign team works out."

That will be a topic for another chapter!

Key Learnings

- *Meetings are where your leadership is on display.*

- *Ensure your meetings have a clear reason to happen, have an intended outcome, and only involve the people who need to be there.*

- *Create engaging meeting invitations, have clear agendas, run meetings on time, and have good meeting record keeping.*

- *Have clear rules on meeting behaviour and decision making, which are consistently enforced.*

- *Enlist the help of others to run the meeting well.*

- *For virtual meetings, have all the requirements of in-person meetings in place but leave some extra space for personal interaction and support.*

- *Openly acknowledge high emotions in meetings while being firm on what is acceptable behaviour.*

- *Do not tolerate poor meeting behaviour; manage it.*

FURTHER READING

Planning the Meeting, Running the Meeting, after the Meeting, before the Next Meeting

Cameron Harold, *Meetings Suck. Turning One of the Most Loathed Elements of Business into One of the Most Valuable* (Muskego, Wisconsin: Lioncrest, 2016).

Antony Jay, "How to Run a Meeting," *Harvard Business Review,* 54, March–April (1976): 43–57.

Monica Olsen and Mary T. Yates, "Designing Engaging and Productive Meetings," *Canadian Journal of Physician Leadership,* 1, Issue 3 (2015):1 6–19.

Monica Olsen and Mary T. Yates, "Keeping the Discussion on Track," *Canadian Journal of Physician Leadership,* 1, Issue 4 (2015): 14–19.

Virtual Meetings

Jeremy N. Bailenson, "Nonverbal Overload: A Theoretical Argument for the Causes of Zoom Fatigue. Technology," *Mind and Behaviour,* 1, Issue 3 (2021): 1–13.

Handling Poor Meeting Behaviour

Nale Lehman-Willenbrock, Joseph A. Allen, and Dain Belyeu, "Our Love/Hate Relationship with Meetings. Relating Good and Bad Meeting Behaviours to Meeting Outcomes, Engagement and Exhaustion," *Management Research Review,* 39 (2016): 1293–1312.

Monica Olsen and Mary T. Yates, "Managing the Behaviour of Challenging Team Members," *Canadian Journal of Physician Leadership,* 2 (2015): 37–41.

John E. Jones, "Dealing with Disruptive Individuals in Meetings," *The 1980 Annual Handbook for Group Facilitators,* ed. J.W. Pfeiffer, (Hoboken, NJ: John Wiley and Sons, 1980): 161–3.

HOW DO I GET OTHER PEOPLE TO DO STUFF?

The second Medical Advisory Committee that Sanjay has attended as Medicine Department Head is just wrapping up. There was an in-depth presentation from the Department Head of Diagnostic Imaging on various activities, initiatives, and challenges in his department. That department is about two thirds the size of Sanjay's. Sanjay is a bit envious of how they seem to have active quality projects going in several areas, a very active journal club, and a well-used continuing education program. They have also been very successful at recruitment to replace several members approaching retirement. Despite this level of activity, Dave, the Department Head, always seems relaxed and in control. Hoping for some tips, Sanjay corners Dave in the car park.

"Dave, that was a great presentation. As you know, I'm kind of new at this, and I was wondering how you manage to juggle all those projects?"

Dave looks a bit puzzled. "I'm not quite sure what you mean. Those are department projects, not mine. I did include who was leading each one in the presentation."

"But surely you're still leading them. I mean, you're accountable for all that stuff as department head."

"Yeah, it's my job to see these things get done, but that doesn't mean I have to do them. I've got good people in the department, most of whom are probably better at what they're doing in those projects than I would be."

Sanjay sighs. "You don't want to send a few of them my way, do you?"

"Are you sure you don't have some already?" Jim replies. "Have you asked?"

"I've certainly put the word out on what we need to do."

"Hmmm, that's not quite the same thing. Tell you what, I must run to pick up my kids now, but I'm in house reading CTs all this week. Why don't you just drop by when you get a minute, and we can compare notes."

In an earlier chapter, I emphasized the importance of securing the support of followers. The reputation of a leader largely rests on the achievements of the group or organization under their leadership. The impact of their leadership is largely through the action of their followers. If, however, those followers are merely a cheerleading squad for the leader, who is left doing all the work, there seems little point to leadership. Yet many leaders set themselves up for just this scenario. How often have you heard "It's just easier to do it myself?" In the short term, sometimes that might be true. But if you choose that course, you're condemning yourself to walk that road forever. Hoarding the work does nothing to build capacity in your group. It influences culture by normalizing a lack of expectation of stepping up and taking responsibility. For a leader, it's a spectacular act of self sabotage. In coaching conversations, it's been my experience that most physician leaders recognize that this behaviour is shooting themselves in the foot, but they can't seem to help themselves. Three themes emerge when one explores why this behaviour is so pervasive:

- **I'm not comfortable asking** - Leaders are uncomfortable "imposing" on busy peers and other individuals and are anxious about pushback or resentment.

- **I'm not sure someone else can do this** - Leaders don't have a system for matching tasks to interests and skills, or they don't have a means for cataloguing skills in their group. They're concerned that delegating the task increases the risk of failure. They're unable to bring themselves to risk trusting their followers.

- **I don't want to lose control over this** - Leaders are uncomfortable ceding control while remaining accountable for success.

This isn't rocket science. Holding on to the work is a burden, but in several ways, it may reduce anxiety in the short term. Our brains love to reduce anxiety. The more often you reduce anxiety this way, the more you reinforce the behaviour. A more sustainable approach is to learn to trust your ability to recruit others to the cause. In this chapter, I'll look at developing that self-trust in four steps: knowing what not to delegate, making the ask, motivating others, and the technical process of delegation.

Knowing What Not to Delegate

While it's true that many leaders set themselves up to fail by not delegating appropriately or enough, delegating unwisely can also have serious consequences. Each task needs a thoughtful decision about whether to hold it or pass it on, but the following categories warrant very careful consideration:

- **Where delegating may represent a breach of a trust or a confidence** - Where the information around an issue is sensitive or embargoed in some way, the task cannot be delegated unless the person is already a member of the circle of trust. Recruiting someone into the trusted environment for the purpose of the task should only be done if all stakeholders, including those who might be affected by a privacy breach, agree.

- **When the decision/policy belongs to you** - Where policy mandates that the decision rests with you, you cannot delegate it. There may be elements necessary to come to a decision that can be delegated. Data gathering, analysis, piloting programs, or processes are examples of things you may be able to entrust to others in a decision-making process. If you do this, you must be clear with those to whom you delegate where their responsibilities end and yours begin.

- **When your presence really matters** - Where something is critically important to a group or organization, the leader needs to be visible. Delegating in this situation can send the wrong signal about your priorities. Seeking support for a new program from a Board or Executive group would be a relevant example. Physician recruitment, particularly of millennials who factor leadership qualities of integrity, mentorship, and collaboration into their decisions, is now an area where physician leaders need to be on deck. Acknowledging and appreciating your followers is also a personal task. I once saw an organization that decided it was time to acknowledge the contribution of medical staff who had provided many years of service. An administrative assistant was assigned to send a paperweight with a slip of paper with the same typed message from the CEO to the relevant physicians. The effect on physician engagement was exactly the reverse of what was intended. A simple phone call from the CEO thanking them would have been much more effective.

- **When in crisis** - You can find examples in any newsfeed of leaders whose standing and reputation is enhanced by their response to a crisis. You can also find examples of reputations that are profoundly diminished. Consider who of these leaders was "front and centre" accepting responsibility and acting, and who was looking around for people to share the pain and the blame. "Command and control" is not the best leadership style for all situations, but it's often appropriate in a crisis. Whether it's a system crisis, such as the many created by the COVID-19 pandemic, or a personal crisis, such as a health or mental-health emergency for a member of your team, this is a part of your leadership job that you own.

Making the Ask

Failing to ask someone to take on a task makes it almost certain that they won't do it, barring a faint hope that they'll suddenly volunteer. When confronted with their failure to ask other physicians to step up, physician leaders bemoan that their colleagues are busy, stressed, have many other commitments, may not be engaged enough, may despise administrative work, and so forth. Often the tasks that they're not being asked to do are mandated under medical staff or clinic bylaws as part of the conditions of practice. In the opening chapter, we talked about boundaries. We described the issue of fusion when boundaries are too permeable. We fuse when we start taking responsibility for other people's experience or blame them for our own. The situation described above is textbook fusion. The leader has a responsibility to get a need of the group met. Meeting that need may not, at least at first, be seen as a positive experience by the person(s) being approached. That's not the leader's problem. The leader may need to listen to concerns and problem solve barriers to participation. That would be an appropriate differentiated leader response. But to avoid asking because the person asked might not like it is not.

You can, however, use some strategy to make the ask more palatable. The following are some suggestions for creating a dialogue around the ask. You may find it helpful to think of something you need to get someone to do. Get a sheet of paper, and after reading each of the bullet points below, write some notes on how you will apply it to the ask you need to make.

- **First, engage!** - Remember the elements of engagement from Michael Bungay Stanier's TERA model we mentioned in a previous chapter (Tribe or group connections, Expectations, Rank or status, Autonomy). It's important to practise engagement at every opportunity, whether you need something from your followers or not. The alternative, turning on the charm only when something needs to be done, will quickly make your followers cynical.

- **Paint the big picture before making the ask** - Describe the issue before making the request to the person/group. Why is it important? How will achieving it serve the collective good of the group? How will achieving it serve the personal good of the person(s) being asked?

- **Be specific and honest about what you are asking** - As much as possible, identify the specific task to be accomplished, the time frame, the resources currently in place and what might become available, and potential barriers and challenges, if known. Be specific as to why you're approaching this person or group. Be sincere and realistic, and do not flatter.

- **Don't open your ask as a "yes/no" question** - Asking, "Will you do it?" helps only if they say yes. Arguing with a "no" risks disengagement with them. A better opening question is "What would you need to come on board on this?" or words to that effect. Whatever answer they give is likely to be informative. Even if they reply, "I don't think I can at the moment," asking a follow-up question—"What's standing in the way for you?"—sounds much more like a natural follow-on question than an argument with their decision. If you can anticipate probable concerns, have ideas for mitigating obstacles ready. Otherwise, be prepared to listen and problem solve.

- **Be prepared for indecision** - If they won't commit one way or the other, make a firm date for a follow-up conversation.

- **Don't ask if there is no choice** - The only thing worse for engagement than having no autonomy is to pretend there is autonomy when there is not. If this a command and not a request, don't pretend to ask. The damage you do by being disingenuous will haunt you for a long time. If there's no choice, go directly to starting the delegation process described later in this chapter.

Motivating Others

For most of the twentieth century, motivation in the workplace involved paying people to do what they were told. This model doesn't work for physician leaders. You're usually leading in an environment where your followers and their families' material survival does not depend on staying in your good graces. In most environments, physicians have many professional options, so reward/coercion systems have little traction. There's also a large body of research that demonstrates that "carrot and stick" systems, known as extrinsic motivation, aren't very effective at getting the best results, particularly when the work requires significant creativity and initiative. Alternatively, a task may align strongly with an individual's intangible needs and personal goals. If circumstances permit, they would do it willingly and without reward. The motivation that drives this behaviour is called intrinsic motivation. Research has shown that intrinsic motivation is associated with much better results in complex, creative, and adaptive tasks. Research has also shown that turning such tasks into paid work often kills rather than reinforces intrinsic motivation. This field is very well reviewed in Daniel Pink's book *Drive* (see "Further Reading" list at the end of this chapter).

Physician leaders are particularly well advised to always start from a position of reinforcing intrinsic motivation before trying extrinsic motivation. The physical needs of the people they are trying to recruit have usually been met. The tasks for which they are recruiting are often complex and cognitively demanding. The person recruited needs to be inspired and creative, both states better served by intrinsic motivation. There are few steps that will help with this.

- **Align task with passion** - The person who is always suggesting system improvements may be your natural lead for a quality initiative. Pay attention to what people are bringing to conversations and use that information in targeting your delegation.

- **Make the task an achievement** - In an earlier chapter, we talked about aligning leadership roles with the components of positive self-determination, autonomy, competence, and relatedness. The same approach is useful here. Present the task in a way that demonstrates how performing it will give the person an increased sense of control in their environment. Identify the skills they may develop or demonstrate. Show the new human connections that can arise or what existing ones will be strengthened.

- **Leverage other passions** - If the task isn't exactly in someone's wheelhouse, is there a way of building something into it that does align for them? For example, you want someone to do a specific quality project. The person you have in mind isn't that enthusiastic about that type of work but loves working with students and trainees. Can you get an educational organization to support you in making the project a trainee exercise for your reluctant candidate to supervise?

Is there any place for tangible rewards in the exercise of physician leadership? Straight extra payment for extra work seems like a simple and straightforward way to proceed. Unfortunately, it becomes the most complex approach. At the level of the brain, pathways of threat perception in the sympathetic nervous system and pathways of reward, known as the mesolimbic dopamine system, are uncomfortably close in their relationship and interconnections. Both are old systems in evolutionary terms and ready to hijack more recent higher thinking processes. Research has shown that monetary reward systems work in the same neural pathways as other reward systems, including drugs. The busy schedules of physicians, the creation of an instant-access culture, and the commoditization of healthcare as a service rather than a set of relationships has made it harder for professionals in this area to be appreciated for who they are and what they do. If the work environment doesn't provide much positive gratification other than money, money may become the main type of reward in their professional life. Instead of being a means, it becomes the end. Using money as the main incentive to recruit creative professionals to additional work in such an environment can create three important problems. Firstly, administrative tasks are often not remunerated at the same level as clinical work. Offering payment that may be perceived as reduced, or being unable to sustain payment past a certain time point, triggers anger. This will erode engagement and group morale. There are excellent videos in the TED system by primatologist Frans de Waal that demonstrate the hardwired nature of this response in capuchin monkeys. We still share the part of the brain that controls this behaviour with them, largely unchanged.

The next problem is that to maintain the same level of satisfaction with the reward over time (the "hit," if you like), ever bigger stimuli are required. In this case, this means more money. This is the same as a cocaine addict needing to snort more and more lines of drug to get the same feeling, which is regulated by the amount of dopamine released by the reward pathway.

Finally, the pursuit of reward (money) may eventually overwhelm other needs, even against self interest and wellbeing. As a physician leader, I've had the experience on more than one occasion of physicians with seven-figure annual net incomes saying to me, "My life is crap (true). I need more money (not true)." Paying very busy people to do yet more work is not a sustainable approach. The leader needs to encourage restructuring the work done to fit the needs to be met, within a sustainable life balance.

Tangible rewards can still have some place in motivation in professional environments, when used carefully. Using resources to mitigate sacrifice is worth consideration. Replacing some income that is foregone to do something for the group, even if less than what is lost, sends a message that the person's efforts are recognized. This supports continued engagement in the group. Messaging around such payment needs to be precise about this being recognition, not compensation, to reduce the risk of triggering a fairness/unfairness response by bringing it into the same valuation system as work. Unexpected rewards, like a leader ordering in pizza for an Emergency Room that's having the Saturday from hell, may work well. Clear linkage to unusual circumstances is important with this approach. Other forms of acknowledgment, such as finding some extra administrative support, access to students and interns as project aids, attendance at development events, time off and support for travel to professional meetings, a restaurant gift card for a meal with their partner, or even just a very public thank you in front of valued peers may be useful and appropriate. On very select occasions, it may be worth paying someone "to just get it done." The best conditions for such an approach are that the task is uninspiring and tedious, the situation is unique and very unlikely to repeat, and the situation has a discrete and very firm endpoint. In all other circumstances, the longer road of integrating the task into the usual workflow of the group may be the wiser.

The Technical Process of Delegation

Successful delegation is a process that requires the commitment of time and resources. Done properly, that commitment is far less than would be required for the leader to do the task themselves. Done very well, it increases capacity in followers, and the demand on the leader decreases with time. The five-step model here is based on one proposed by Barbara Linney, a consultant specializing in leadership development at the American Association of Physician Leadership. Other similar models are included in the "Further Reading" section.

The process outlined below begins after you have identified the person(s) to whom the task is being delegated, and you have secured agreement for their participation. Some of what is mentioned below may have come up in your recruitment process. Repetition in the service of achieving clarity is not a bad thing.

- **Be clear and specific on the task, the timeline, and the results required** - Create a written outline (even just in point form) of what needs to be done, and when and why, as a shared starting point for this discussion. Book a time and have this conversation in an undistracted environment. Delegation is not something to be done opportunistically in the coffee-shop line up.

- **Create time and space for the person(s) to discuss their concerns and ideas before the process starts** - This could be part of the meeting above, or if time permits, a second (possibly shorter) meeting before project commencement to allow time for them to think about their approach.

- **Give autonomy while being clear on boundaries** - Conferring some autonomy is a non-negotiable part of motivating others to perform a task on your behalf. Be specific both on where in the process they decide what happens, and the circumstances that should trigger them re-consulting you. If there are interpersonal sensitivities—for example, people who should not be involved in this for whatever reason—make sure they're aware of the specifics. Having established the boundaries, explore if they're comfortable with them. It's possible that the level of autonomy is more than they were expecting, and this may generate anxiety. This may require a more specific conversation about why you feel they're up to the task, why you trust them with this, and perhaps why you're willing to accept the risk of failure. It may require negotiating a bit more support of some kind. Conversely, you need to give them space to express reservations that they're still being overmanaged and explore whether more autonomy might work better for them.

- **Negotiate follow up** - Delegating a task and not monitoring progress is both lazy and foolhardy. As a physician leader, you're almost certainly delegating to a smart, motivated person. You need to develop a follow-up process that respects your need to be informed and to change course, if necessary, without appearing to micromanage them. Having agreed on the framework, commit to it. Book time for first and possibly other follow-up connections in all the relevant calendars at the time of the initial delegation meeting. Impersonal contact such as email and written reports may be appropriate for data, but it's good practice to set aside personal-contact time, even if only by phone, to check in on the experience of the person to whom the task is delegated. Email, at best, will lose its nuances … at worst, it will feed misunderstanding.

- **Give appropriate attention to the person(s) to whom you have delegated** - I have very intentionally used the word "attention" here, not "feedback." Feedback seems to have negative connotations in some quarters as being a tool to manage sub-optimal performance. Attention captures the need to use interactions to not only examine progress and course correct, but to acknowledge the experience of those doing the task, appreciate their input, and celebrate their successes. Obviously, these are the actions of a decent, considerate leader. But they're also essential to the process of embedding the learning that hopefully has occurred during the delegation and performance of the task. Several research studies have concluded that positive appreciation is more than just a carrot that makes people more willing to help you next time. Appreciation is an important part of the organizational learning process and capacity building within complex, high-performing systems.

Go back to the task you identified at the beginning of this chapter and imagine how you will apply these five steps to delegating that task.

If you're interested in knowing where you need to focus your attention within developing your delegation skills, the Mindtools organization has an online assessment you can try. The link can be found in the "Further Reading" section.

Meanwhile, Sanjay is recruiting a new chair for the departmental Quality Committee ...

Sanjay ends up having several chats with Dave in the days that follow and gets several ideas he is now keen to try with his department members. One evening, he calls Louise at home (having asked permission to do so), one of his department members who tends to speak up about measures to improve care.

"Hi, Louise. Thanks for taking my call. Is it still an okay time?"

"Sure, the kids are in bed. I'm a bit intrigued as to what this is about."

"Well, you know we're required by the bylaws to have a Quality Committee. We've gone nearly a year since the previous Chair retired without that group meeting, which means we've sort of stalled on some good ideas in the pipeline. Not to mention that we're delinquent in doing our mortality and morbidity rounds."

"I was wondering when that would get going again."

"I've noticed that, at our department meetings, you step up with ideas when issues of care needing to be done better come up. I'm not the only who has noticed. Several other people, both in the department and in hospital administration, have been asking me if this is something you're interested in."

"Is that a question?"

"Well, yes, I suppose it is."

"I am interested. I like to think I, or we, are always doing the best we can for patients, but realistically, there's always room to improve. I did some projects in quality improvement in my residency, even got a couple published, but I've sort of let it slide behind other commitments since then."

"Here's the thing. That committee has been drifting a bit for years now, and the three members left on it are all talking about retirement in the near future. We need to get it back up to about five physicians. In addition to new physician blood, I'd like to get some non-physician input on it as well."

"Sounds fair. I'd say the last part, getting the staff that work with our patients involved, is critical. I'm a bit surprised it wasn't set up that way in the first place."

"In fact, it was seen as a 'doctors' committee.' You're right, that doesn't fit with the way the organization wants us to approach quality and safety issues, but that's another reason none of the existing members have stepped up. Managing that change, which has to happen, is a bit of a step too far for them."

Louise sighs. "I could see that."

Sanjay makes his move. "So, we need someone to take on that group who cares about quality of care and patient safety and is keen to work in an interdisciplinary fashion in that cause. We have a lot of new blood in the department and the staff, with more coming, so I think this is going to be one of the areas where our department can really take off and do some great stuff. I'm really hoping we can use Quality as a way of strengthening or rebuilding connections with other departments. I'll be honest, yours is the name that has come up most often by far. Your interest in this area has certainly been recognized. There's a strong feeling that you have great skills in working with teams that we're not using to your full potential. What do you need to consider becoming Chair of the Quality Committee?"

"This is bit sudden. I think I'd need to think about it."

"Fair enough. But what comes immediately to mind that I could be looking at?"

"Well, obviously I have two young kids, so I'm wary of anything that adds to time away from home, so if I took this on, something else would have to go. We're now committed to some serious house renos, so I don't want to cut into my clinical income at the moment, so it would probably need to be other committee work, like the residency committee, for example."

"Okay. I think I know someone who might be willing to take on the residency committee. This job does come with a stipend, admittedly a very small one, as a gesture more than anything else, but it will pay for something on the *reno! Other departments have had no trouble getting medical association grants to support Quality Chairs going to relevant meetings and courses, including the IHI conference each year in Orlando. You could piggyback on a Disney World trip for the kids."*

"My, you are trying to sell it. I think they're still a bit young for Disney World. But okay, I will seriously think about it. When do you need to know?"

"I'd like to settle this in the next couple of weeks. Could we perhaps chat again over coffee before clinic in the next two or three days to put some more flesh on these bones? Say, Friday?"

"Sure. See you then. Say hi to Evelyn for me. And by the way, any of your kids getting close to babysitting age?"

"I will. And yes, our eldest is doing the course at school next month."

"Hmmm. That may be part of my price. See you Friday!"

Key Learnings

- *Getting the best from others is the prime role of leadership.*

- *Be clear on what can be delegated and what must be held by the leader.*

- *Build on engagement skills to develop a process for asking others to move outside their comfort zones.*

- *Align what you ask of others with their passions and skills.*

- *Appeal to intrinsic motivation before offering tangible rewards. Delegate tasks in a way that allows your followers to demonstrate or acquire new skills, develop new relationships, and become more independent.*

- *Use delegation to build the capacity of your team.*

- *Put aside adequate time for the steps of delegation:*
    - *achieving clarity on the task*
    - *discussing concerns and strategy*
    - *understanding autonomy and limits*
    - *scheduling follow up*
    - *giving recognition of achievements.*

FURTHER READING

Motivating Others

Daniel H. Pink, *Drive. The Surprising Truth about What Motivates Us* (New York, NY: Riverhead Books, 2009).

Frans de Waal, "Moral Behavior in Animals," *TED Ideas Worth Spreading,* August 18, 2021, https://www.ted.com/talks/ frans_de_waal_moral_behavior_in_animals?language=en.

The Technical Process of Delegation

Barbara J. Linney, "The Art of Delegation," *Physician Executive,* 24 (1998): 58–63.

"8 Steps of Effective Delegation," *Physician Leadership Journal,* 7 (2020): 88.

Carla L. Brown, *Essential Delegation Skills* (London: Routledge, 1997).

Mindtools Content Team, "Using the Power of Other People's Help," July 15, 2021, https://www.mindtools.com/pages/article/newLDR_98.htm.

WE NEED TO TALK

Rosalind comes into her office after lunch and sees a sticky note stuck to her computer screen: "Hi, Rosalind, sorry I missed you. Could you give me a call at your earliest convenience? Mark (Human Resources)."

Rosalind is a bit puzzled and a bit apprehensive, wondering what warrants an unannounced personal visit rather than an email. She manages to connect with him later that afternoon.

Mark thanks her for calling and then pauses. "How well do you know Dr. Smith in Psychiatry?"

Rosalind thinks for a second. "I know who he is, but I don't think I've spoken to him much other than around a couple of psych consults in the Emergency Department."

"What's your impression of him?"

"I don't know. Seemed a pleasant enough, competent guy. Like I said, he hasn't really come up on my radar. What's your interest in him?"

"I had a rather concerning call from the Outpatient Mental Health services manager about him. She has received three complaints from staff about abusive outbursts in the last week. One staff member was reduced to tears. She's considering a formal complaint of bullying. The manager is pretty concerned about her staff, but she's also a bit worried about Dr. Smith. She made a comment that they're used to 'personalities' down there, but this isn't like him. She did try to reach out to him, and he told her to mind her own business. She was quite surprised he was that blunt, and frankly, rude."

"It certainly doesn't sound good. How can I help?"

"Someone is going to have to talk to him. If the employee does file a formal complaint of bullying, workplace legislation will require us to do a formal investigation. My hope is that we can get to the bottom of this and secure

a less formal resolution before it gets that far. I would have approached his department head, but he's on an extended vacation in Europe, and the person acting shares a private office with Dr. Smith, which could make it difficult. So, I'm coming to you."

Rosalind's stomach begins to knot. She'd known that it was just a matter of time before she would have a conversation like this with somebody, but Dr. Smith is a senior physician. She's also a bit intimidated by the idea of verbal fencing about behaviour with an experienced psychiatrist. "Thanks, Mark. Can you send me a copy of the manager's complaint and any other relevant documentation? I'll reach out to him as soon as possible."

She ends the call and takes a deep breath. She then picks up the phone and calls Jim, the regional medical director ...

Managing significant conversations is the most common issue raised by physician leadership clients in my coaching practice. For those in, and particularly those new to, physician leadership positions, the most common type of conversation they bring into coaching is one they are facing about the behaviour or performance of another physician or healthcare professional. Confronting such conversations with peers causes everything from mild anxiety to serious distress. I also sometimes coach people who are on the receiving end of such conversations. They face similar emotional turmoil. This is, however, just one example of a conversation in which there is a pressing need for two or more people to clearly communicate their experience of a situation and work to find a common path forward. The ideas and approaches you will sample in this chapter can be used in any situation where the conversation really matters. Whether you're advocating to leadership for a new program, exploring treatment options with a patient, or negotiating curfew with teenage children, I believe you'll find things here that are of value.

Stories, Models, and Maps

At the heart of effective communication is the distinction between what is happening in the physical world and what we, as cognitive beings, experience. Put bluntly, our responses in the moment are shaped not by what is happening but by what we *think* is happening. This means we all experience a particular event differently. We build elaborate constructions to characterize our reality. These constructions about how our world works are guided by our need to make sense of the world. They're influenced by other experiences, what we already believe, and what we feel. These constructions then feed back into the shaping of our experiences.

The term "mental maps" is sometimes used as a visual representation of how we see some part of our world. This concept originated in work with rats in mazes, but now several concepts of thought claim the "map" term with somewhat different meanings, so I'll stick with "models." Unfortunately, we often forget that our experience of the world is subjective and prone to misinterpretation. We see the models we build as our reality, our truth, if you prefer, and we often defend them to the death. We build our models whether we have lots of information or very little. Based as they are on incorrect or inadequate information, these constructions are often wrong. We can, however, choose to be aware of the risks and treat our own constructions with an appropriate degree of skepticism. In effect, we can treat them as workable theories rather than fact. In being skeptical about our own models, we must admit that other models could be as valid, or more so, than ours. This requires that we treat each other's models with respect and curiosity rather than disdain.

Another widely used term for these constructions is "stories." These stories contain the settings of our experience; the roles, characteristics, behaviours, and motivations of the main players; and our place in the story. Success is not proving one story correct and another wrong. Success in a significant conversation is achieving understanding of each other's story, model, or map, and then being able to collaborate on a new story that meets more of the needs of all parties.

Several authors have proposed approaches to creating and sharing narratives around experience. Most of this work refers to publications by Dr. Cristopher Argyris. Argyris made many leading contributions to the fields of organizational development and understanding of organizational behaviour, but the one most relevant here is the Ladder of Inference. He proposed a four-rung ladder by which observable data from the real world translates into human experience. He proposed the data (rung 1) is filtered through cultural meaning (rung 2) and then personal meaning (rung 3) to produce theories (rung 4) that in turn feed back to shape and adjust personal meaning. This popular concept has been extensively used and refined over the last four decades to a more complex ladder, such as is shown in Figure 5. We all use the Ladder of Inference, mostly without any awareness that we have rushed up the ladder to a questionable conclusion that we now accept as truth.

Argyris referred to mental models as theories of action. In his research, he noted that the theories of action described by leaders (called "espoused theories") versus what they did (called "theories-in-use") were often different. He also underlined the common tendency for conversations to be quite disconnected from the thoughts and feelings of the participants. This can be further complicated by observations from research by Michael Gazzaniga and colleagues. Over several decades, they studied people whose brains had been surgically divided so that communication between the hemispheres of the brain was interrupted. They found that the left hemisphere of the brain has an "interpreter" that will create narratives for actions of the other hemisphere. When the left hemisphere doesn't receive the input that caused the other half of the brain to act, due to the cutting of the connections between the two, it has no knowledge of the reason for the action. The "interpreter" then simply creates a story that explains the action, which the owner of the brain believes to be true. In short, if our story has holes in it, we have a brain area dedicated to filling in the blanks. We may not be able to tell the difference between the parts of the story that happened and those our brain created in search of consistency.

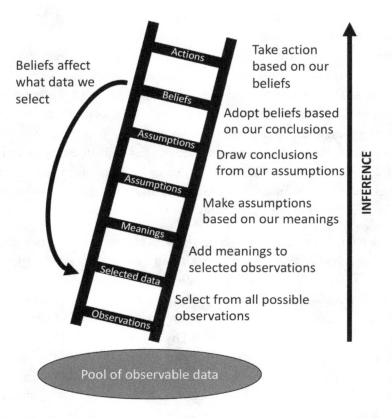

Figure 5. *The Ladder of Inference (after Argyris, C. [1982])*

This phenomenon, known as confabulation, is common in severe alcoholic brain damage and other forms of dementia. But this pathological storytelling is merely an uncontrolled example of a tendency that we all innately possess. Let's apply the Ladder of Inference to what Rosalind knows so far about Dr. Smith. Say Rosalind has a few run-ins with some of the older physicians. She develops a story that they have issues with her age, gender, and lifestyle choices. She selects from the data Dr. Smith's age and seniority and his unacceptable behaviour in making staff cry. She begins to form a story about conservatism, old school hierarchical thinking, arrogance, and lack of empathy. She picks up on the fact that his department head is away and starts adding a dimension about him having the gall to think he can get away with it when the boss is away. He has another thing coming! But what if her attention is on the fact that the clinic manager is a bit concerned about him and sees this as atypical behaviour. She then constructs a possible story that there is something amiss in his life. Is he now an aging physician showing an early sign of dementia? Does he need help? Does the old guard culture to which he belongs make it hard for him to seek that help? Is he even aware of what he's doing? Same observations—very different story.

The stories that generate the most anxiety for leaders are almost always stories about people and relationships. This adds another, often unhelpful, dimension to the stories that can influence behaviour—the Drama Triangle. This idea was introduced over fifty years ago by psychiatrist Stephen Karpman. Karpman saw dysfunctional relationships consisting of three roles that people might adopt at different times in the relationship: victim, rescuer (or hero), and persecutor (or villain). Remember the old silent movie meme of a damsel in distress tied up on a railway line by a dastardly villain, only to be rescued in the nick of time by the plucky cowboy, or a frozen and incapacitated Han Solo in the palace of Jabba the Hutt being rescued by Princess Leia in *Star Wars*? It turns out that this structure comes from more than a flash of a screenwriter's imagination. It turns up repeatedly in all human systems.

When we're unhappy about something, we tend to adjust the settings on our Ladder of Inference to generate a story that makes us the victim and someone else the persecutor. Leaders often find themselves cast as the rescuer or hero. Well, that sounds like a good place to be in the story, does it not? In fact, no. This is a trap for the leader. When the leader gets pulled into rescuing, what's often happening is that they feel bad about the person's experience. They often rescue the person so that they, the leader themselves, can feel better. Remember fusion? It's at work again here. Rescuing behaviour as a way of managing leader anxiety can become ingrained or addictive to the point of being pathological. In rescuing the person, the leader has failed to help them become capable of solving their own problems. There may be times when a leader makes a conscious decision that rescue is the best option. After all, people do like to be thought of as caring. A caring response is deliberate, where the consequences of the leader's action are weighed against any potential downside. A fused response is spontaneous, where the leader just reacts and begins the rescue. The leader who rescues without thinking of the consequences may create a demand for rescue so great that they themselves will burnout under the load. Carrying everyone's burdens in a group or organization is rarely sustainable. If the leader reaches that point and rescues themselves by suddenly no longer rescuing their followers, they now become the villain. Leaders must watch for and avoid the Drama Triangle trap in the significant conversations they join. Help people solve their own problems, but don't just rescue them. Get them to rewrite their stories so that they claim the hero role for themselves.

Bias and Prejudice – The Dark Side of Mental Models

We have established that how a situation is perceived depends upon the filters of someone's beliefs and experiences. The harsh fact is that many of those beliefs are beyond a leader's control. The growing strength of the equity and diversity movement has underscored the operation of bias and prejudice in healthcare leadership selection and the experience of healthcare leaders. There's already a strong movement advocating around gender disparity in physician and healthcare leadership. Publications exploring the experience of physicians from racial minorities are fewer, and those of LGBTQ physicians are rare. What is available suggests that the experience of physicians from these minorities is often as distressing as that of others in these groups who have been more in the public eye. Much work still needs to be done exploring and mitigating bias and prejudice in medical leadership. Someone with overt prejudice or strong unconscious bias against some characteristic of a leader will set a much higher bar for credibility and performance. Conversely, a leader with such unconscious bias may be less prone to give someone who triggers that bias the benefit of the doubt. They be more prone to set differing standards amongst their followers. Nor can we assume the direction our unconscious bias takes. If we are raised in an environment that builds negative associations towards groups with whom we identify, it is not rare to have unconscious bias against people like ourselves.

Such beliefs cannot be changed easily or quickly; they are deeply rooted in the psyche. While the actions of overtly prejudicial groups may be obvious, unconscious bias, quietly and inexorably shaped by our life experience, is likely a much more powerful force. Project Implicit, a collaboration between researchers at several universities and operating out of Harvard, provides free assessments of implicit or unconscious bias while gathering a vast database for research in this area. You can find the link to the online tests to evaluate your own implicit biases in the "Further Reading" section. Take the test and encourage others around you to do so; the results are often both illuminating and surprising.

Recent authors on this topic have suggested that one-on-one conversations may be of limited practical impact due to the strong subconscious nature of these biases. Systemic measures to contain and reduce the influence of these prejudices are the preferred strategy. Driving system change is covered in a later chapter.

Setting the Stage

Significant conversations go better with planning, even if that planning is just a contingency for a conversation only if the opportunity arises. Much of setting the stage for a significant or challenging conversation is simply being intentional about engaging the other person. There are a few things to consider in preparing for an important conversation.

- **Place** - Place and meaning are often intertwined. Being summonsed to an administrative office commonly draws comments of "being sent to the principal's office," with all the baggage that comes with that. Using neutral and (if appropriate) informal locations can help start the conversation on an even, or at least less threatening, basis. Consider the layout. The most effective conversations are about talking *with* someone, not *at* them. Does the furniture create that collegial effect, or are there "battle lines" drawn in wood, plastic, or steel between you? When things get tense, people may need physical space to pull back and feel less threatened. Does your space have them backed into a corner right from the start, or is there room for them to control their personal space?

- **Time** - A later chapter explores concepts in time management and planning in more detail, but it's worth a mention in this context. With busy schedules, negotiating a time is often challenging, but making reasonable efforts to find the least inconvenient time will remove one more stressor and distraction. Practical issues aside, it's also important to recognize that we function differently at different times of the day. There's a general principle that we have peaks in our ability to perform analytically and logically, which for most people are in the morning and early evening. We have troughs when we are furthest from our best game, which for most people are early to mid afternoon. It's more complicated than just being sleepy after a big lunch. Setting up an important conversation for early to mid afternoon may be giving yourself a handicap. The minority of the population who are true night owls can show a reverse pattern, and you may have to take that into account with specific people.

- **Framing the topic** - A useful concept that comes from the very popular "Crucial Conversations" program created by Kerry Patterson, Joseph Grenny, Ron McMillan, and Al Switzler is Mutual Purpose. Is there an element or outcome in the situation to be discussed on which both or all parties already agree? Using Rosalind's upcoming conversation as an example again, she could call Dr. Smith and say, "Hi, Dr. Smith. I've had complaints about you yelling at the staff. We need to talk." This will have him reaching for his armour and weapons before he's put the phone down. Or she could say, "Hi, Dr. Smith. I'm calling you about something that has come up through human resources around our requirement to have a respectful workplace. They've been made aware of some incidents in which staff in the mental health clinic feel their experience hasn't been meeting the standard. I've been told that these incidents included you, and I need to hear your perspective to help me respond to HR and work with them to bring us back to where we need to be on this."

Certainly, Dr. Smith will know the conversation is not likely about giving him a medal for his behaviour. The conversation, however, is now about "we need a respectful workplace," hopefully something that isn't particularly controversial in the twenty-first century. No longer is it being framed as a retaliatory strike on Dr. Smith. Where you have more detailed knowledge of the hopes, goals, and values of the other parties in a conversation, you may well be able to come up with even more sophisticated ways of framing the start of the conversation around a point of agreement. Performance or behaviour conversations such as Rosalind's with Dr. Smith are also at great risk of invoking shame. Shame can be considered as the state in which we are confronted within our own minds with a negative image of ourselves of our own creation. This is different from guilt, where we feel we have *done* something bad; shame says *we are bad*. The two states can certainly co-exist. Shame stimulates strong negative emotions and very quickly puts people into fight or flight. This makes them far less receptive to a thoughtful exchange of ideas. One way of approaching this is to frame the conversation around a gap or discrepancy. Rosalind's hypothetical response above is an example of this. She has identified an expected standard and an incident that falls below that standard, so she expresses curiosity about the gap. Her statement makes no assumption about Dr. Smith's character.

- **Engage, engage, engage** - This keeps coming up. Whether you set up a meeting with a phone call (usually strongly advised for disciplinary/performance meetings) or a written invitation, thinking about engagement at every step is crucial. Right from the start in setting up your conversation, emphasize group connection, set clear expectations, affirm rank or status, and create space for autonomy. Where things could get off the rails during the conversation, working to establish a group connection has an additional benefit. If someone from my ingroup does something undesirable, I'm likely to ascribe it to the circumstances at the time. I view it as a transient aberration. If, on the other hand, the same offence is committed by someone outside the group, that now underlines their defective character and reinforces why I am not in a group with them. Being in-group might get you a pass on a misstep or two. Once the conversation is underway, you still need to be practising these concepts. With Rosalind's conversation, she might continue her invitation call with something like the following:

"Dr. Smith, all of us on the medical staff benefit from a workplace where people feel safe and confident to contribute. I remember you spoke in support of this at the annual meeting. I was very encouraged by your support then (Tribe/group). I need this meeting to get a clear picture of what's been happening in the clinic. There have been complaints, but at this stage no one is making it formal, so my hope is that we can come to an understanding about whatever the issues are and problem solve without getting into a formal process (Expectations). You're a very senior and valued member of the medical staff, and I'm confident you can bring some valuable insights to this (Rank/status). It's important we do this soon, as I'm concerned that, if we don't address this promptly, we'll encourage stories to circulate that may be detrimental to relationships in the clinic. That said, I know your schedule may be more difficult to juggle than mine, so if it's in the next week (setting a clear boundary), I'm happy to try to fit with your schedule. Likewise, we could meet in my office, or if there's somewhere on the premises that works better for you, I can come there. Happy to bring coffee! (Autonomy)."

Prepare for Emotion, Yours and Theirs

Emotion is intrinsic to human interaction, so it needs to be factored into significant conversation planning. Emotions can be stimulated almost instantaneously and involuntarily by incoming sensory input. A term that often comes up in this context is "controlling" emotion, usually in the context of "negative" emotional states like anger, fear, or anxiety. Emotions are not synthesized or amenable to conscious control; they just happen. We can, however, choose to be aware of our emotions and choose to control our behaviour in response to those emotions. There are a few practices that can help in this area.

- **Know your triggers** - Anyone working in conflict resolution or coaching will tell you that the gut-wrenching experience of being in conflict does not come from simple disagreement. It comes from perceiving an assault on our basic needs, our identity as a person or as part of our tribe, or on our dearly held values. Can you anticipate where that might happen and be prepared to manage your behaviour? Rosalind, for example, in her interaction with Dr. Smith, might consider how she will respond if he lashes out at her age, gender, the fact that she's in a same sex-relationship, or her competence as Chief of Staff or even just as a physician.

- **Know when you're triggered** - Emotions are intimately linked to the physiology of our autonomic nervous system, the operating system that keeps our bodies working and in balance. As a result, emotional states are always associated with actual bodily sensations, commonly regional in nature: like a tightening in the chest, tensing of muscles, or strange feeling in the abdomen. The exact nature of these is part of our own unique experience and is different for us all. Be aware of what it feels like when you're getting angry, scared, sad, defensive, and so forth so that you can go into a behavioural control strategy for your emotional state sooner rather than later.

- **Have a plan for when you are triggered** - This is one with which you can have some fun. Practise (with a very trusted person!) being triggered and see what works to keep your behaviour under control. It could be something as simple as a short breathing exercise in the mindfulness vein to give you time to acknowledge the emotion and let the edge of it pass. It could be having someone in the meeting who can recognize your warning signs and introduce a distraction. It could be bringing a description of your emotional state into the conversation.

What of the other person? They will likely be having just as rich and varied an emotional experience in the meeting as you are. The bad news is that there is only one thing you can do with the emotions of others. Fortunately, it's a very powerful thing. You can acknowledge them. Acknowledging means being aware and telling them you are aware. The first part of this is easy. It's yet another one of those things we can't help doing. Our brains include a phenomenon called "mirror neurons." When we perceive something or someone else doing or experiencing something, mirror neurons will fire in a pattern as if we were doing or experiencing that same thing ourselves. The term is a bit deceiving, as it implies the odd cell firing off here and there, when it's often whole complex pathways activating. Have you ever cried, or tried not to, at a sad or happy and uplifting movie? Have you ever started having involuntary movements that mimic the action of something exciting you are watching? Film makers are experts at this. Think back on a thriller or horror movie that really scared you. You'll probably find the scariest bits weren't the things that go bump in the night but when you were watching someone on the screen being really scared. All the above happens because of mirror neurons. Acknowledging the other person's emotion has two benefits. It reduces the level of amygdala activation, and it goes some way to calming their emotional response. This will help them engage with what is happening at a more thoughtful level. Research within a field called "Costly Signalling Theory" also suggests that openly acknowledging the emotion of others increases the probability of trust.

Acknowledging the emotions of others needs to be done with care. You are, after all, guessing what is going on in their heads; you could be wrong. It's prudent to start with what you are noticing and then say what you're inferring from that observation, phrased as a question if possible. For example, "I notice that you are frowning and getting tense. Is this making you angry?" If you're not sure what the signs are saying or just want to tread carefully, you could say, "I'd like to pause for a moment and check in on how this is affecting you. How do you feel right now?"

There's another important caveat with this approach: You *cannot* tell people what they are feeling, and you *must not* tell them what they *should* feel. Particularly in an emotionally charged situation, these behaviours are at best annoying and at worst provocative. Refraining from them takes practice and discipline, because we all tend to do both. We can blurt out a statement about what someone else is feeling simply because we take our impressions and experience as truth. It takes conscious effort to question our own conclusions. If we conclude that someone is feeling bad, we tend to mirror that and feel bad ourselves. The fastest thing we can do to stop ourselves from feeling bad is to tell them to feel something different. Comments like the following may sound sympathetic, but they're not helpful: *"It's not that bad."* Here and now, it is. You're not in their head. How would you know? Try, *"This seems to be hitting you pretty hard. I'm willing to listen if you want to talk about it."*

"There's no reason to be ___ (insert emotion here)." is saying that the person is unreasonable for feeling what they're feeling. Try, *"I'm getting the sense you feel (insert emotion). What's the main thing that's driving that for you?"*

"I know how you feel." You really don't. You are guessing how they feel. Try, *"I can't imagine what that feels like. Would you like to talk about it?"*

"You'll feel better tomorrow." You want to feel better now by pretending their pain will go away very soon. Try, *"This must be tough. Let me know when you're ready to ___ (continue/take next steps). In the interim, is there anything I can do?"*

You get the idea. You're far better off being curious about the emotional impact and then letting the other person(s) describe it and come to any conclusions about the course it should run. They are the owners of their emotional state, not you. Doing this may feel less comfortable in the short run but will avoid long-term relationship damage.

Ground Rules for a Conversation

One of the hazards of significant conversations is that we invest so much energy in preparing for them that we begin to think of just having the conversation as the goal. In fact, the conversation is just another tool to get to a goal. There are a lot of books on having and managing significant conversations. A full discussion of all the options and techniques is beyond the scope of this book, but you'll find some examples of popular approaches in the "Further Reading" section. Several common factors emerge from these different approaches. Some of these we have covered in the preceding sections. A couple of additional important ones are:

- **Know the purpose of the conversation and what you hope to achieve** - This could be one of the factors that distinguishes a significant conversation from normal social intercourse: Something needs to happen. The "something" could be a sharing of information, arrival at an agreement on a concept, or commitment to an action. One approach to this, when you're thinking about having a conversation, is to write the following sentence: *"I will have this conversation to enable___ (insert purpose here)."* Too often, well-meaning people exchange information but walk away without clarity on what must now happen. Conversations are necessary to change the world, but the world-changing events must follow from the conversation rather than occur within it. Achieving clarity on purpose provides a reference point for whether the conversation is on track or not. When something comes into the conversation that seems off course, be prepared to ask the question: *"We're here today to ___ (enter purpose here). Can you help me understand how ___ (whatever has just been introduced) gets us there?"* But don't dismiss attempts to change course out of hand. The other person may have seen something for which you have a blind spot, so asking how it fits shouldn't be a rhetorical question. It should be a sincere request for clarity. Knowing the purpose can also help when someone else in the conversation says something that you perceive as a threat or attack. Rather than withdraw or counterattack, take a moment to reflect, either in your own head or out loud, on the purpose. Then treat your desire to withdraw or retaliate as another distraction. You might respond to a personal attack with, *"I'm sorry that's how you see me, and I'd like to have a conversation about that at another time, but today our task is___"*

- **Tell your experience, but for everything else, ask** - This is about more than asking extremely clever and insightful questions, although that is useful. It's about approaching a significant conversation recognizing that a lot of what you think you "know" about other people and their experience is a collection of assumptions that have been elevated to your mental model of those people. To be sure, there is some technical skill to using questions well, but if you're not genuinely curious and coming from a position that your world view is likely incomplete, there's a good chance you won't focus on the answers you're hearing. Telling people about their experience rather than your own is very disengaging and damaging to trust. This is covered in detail in Judith Glaser's approach to this topic in her book *Conversational Intelligence.*

- **Even if the topic comes from the past, the conversation stays in the now** - When a conversation occurs, anything it produces comes from what happens in that collection of moments. This may seem a bit counterintuitive, as many conversations are about something that has happened in the past. The point is that the past cannot be changed. Past experiences can't be changed; they can only be described. That description, based as it is on memory, may itself not be accurate. What can happen in real time is a sharing, and possibly, gaining some understanding of how an event was experienced. It may be possible to make decisions on actions or process going forward based on that understanding. If your conversation seems to be an exchange of curiosity about some past event that was experienced, and that experience is an influence on current events, you're probably on track. If, on the other hand, your conversation is an argument about what happened in the past, with different sides trying to convince others of what are correct and incorrect versions of history, you're off track. This is time wasted. Often people feel driven to "get to the bottom of it," meaning find the ultimate truth. Not only is that impossible without a time machine but it's also not helpful. This is most apparent in conversations with a significant element of conflict. Historical fact finding is well recognized in mediation practice and conflict coaching as being of little value in contributing to a resolution. Indeed, it may just perpetuate flash points in the conflict. Conflict resolution is more often about finding a new path on which parties can agree than trying to find truth in the old paths.

What can be helpful is recognizing when you're being dragged into unproductive history. When you feel that happen, pull the conversation back into the present and move from debate to design. Imagine that, at some point in Rosalind's conversation with Dr. Smith, she hears his version of events, which turns out to be somewhat different from the reports she has received. She might say, *"Thank you. I think I understand how it looked from where you stand. I think everyone is being truthful about how they experienced what happened, and it's clear there are some very different perceptions about what was happening. We can't go back and change that, but we do need to get back to a place where people in that clinic feel comfortable working together. Do you have any thoughts about how we can do that?"* This keeps the conversation focused in the present and avoids making judgements that will generate defensiveness and hostility.

- **Listen as much or more than you talk** - In 1936, Dale Carnegie introduced the idea of "Levels of Listening" with a five-step model in his iconic book, *How to Win Friends and Influence People*. Since then, and recently with the help of the Internet, hundreds of different "Levels of Listening" articles have emerged, ranging from three to many levels. All are based on some common concepts. The first is the difference between listening and hearing. Without mechanical obstruction to sound, we're unable to stop ourselves hearing. We protect ourselves from this avalanche of data by unconsciously ignoring most of the noise before it reaches awareness. Our precon-scious mind is monitoring that stream of data. Our attention will snap on if we hear our name, or another word or sound that carries a lot of significance. We may be consciously aware of a conversation without really listening to its content. Often, particularly in emo-tionally charged circumstances, we're not looking at the incoming information; we're just looking for a break in the flow so that we can jump in and make our point.

In significant conversations, frequently checking that you can recall what was just said is important to test that your attention is in the right place. Once paying attention, the simplest level of listening is simply working to accurately receive the data. At this level, we focus simply on what is being said. We may test our hearing with repeating it back, either within our thoughts or out loud. At the next level, we listen for the meaning or significance of the language we're hearing in terms of the mental model of the situation being built by the participants. What do the words, intonation, and body language tell us about the different mental models of the partici-pants? Where do they overlap and where do they differ? What is the dialogue telling us about what's happening? What does the information mean to me and others? At the highest levels of listen-ing, we listen for what impact the conversation is having. What's happening for the people taking part? How is this affecting them? Imagine that, at the end of any significant conversation, there will be a test. That test will ask three questions: What was said? What did it mean? What was its impact on us? If you're listening well, you'll be able to provide fulsome answers to all three questions.

The Art of the Question

There are several layers to the construction of helpful questions in sig-nificant conversations. The first, which should be well known to physi-cians, as it's part of basic teaching in medical history taking, is the differ-ence between open and closed questions. "How are you feeling?" is much more likely to generate useful information than "Are you feeling good?" An open question allows the answerer to control the detail and direction of the answer. Closed questions have limited options and are more prone to biased answers. Where there is a finite choice of answers, we risk getting the answer that the person thinks we want, or one that isn't accurate but is perceived as being closest to what the person would like to say. It might not be close enough and could lead to misunderstanding. Another useful way of thinking about questions has been articulated by Edgar and Peter Schein in their book *Humble Inquiry*. They talk about three types of inquiry: diagnostic, confrontive, and process. Diagnostic inquiry aims to steer the conversation in a direction that will contribute to progress on the issue or help the parties involved. Diagnostic questions can be about simply learning more about the topic, learning more about the emotions involved or about actions that have happened or are contemplated. Usually, this should be the most common type of question.

Confrontive questions occur when the asker starts injecting their ideas into the question. *"Why didn't you do* (action) *the following way:* (asker's idea of how it should be done)*?"* Confrontive questions are a favourite tactic in situations where the asker is trying to get a specific answer from somebody. It's probably best to avoid them, at least in normal circumstances, as they can be perceived as threatening and put people on the defensive. There may be a place for them where an asker is meeting stiff resistance to an important concept. But if you do use them as something of a shock tactic, you need to follow up with your engagement skills to soften the landing once your point is made. Trying a phased response is wiser in most circumstances. You could open with *"Can you think of any other options?"* If that doesn't do the trick, try *"This situation makes me wonder about ___* (unrecognized option). *What do you think about that?"* If they still don't take the bait, you might have to go nuclear. You could soften it with a lead up like *"Do you mind if I ask a blunt question?"* But this carries the obvious hazard of them saying, "Yes, I do mind," shooting yourself in the foot. An approach that gets around this would be *"I feel I need to ask you a blunt question at this point."* At least you're acknowledging honestly the effect you might have.

Process questions are specific to what is happening between you: Are we making progress? Is this helpful to you? What are your thoughts about how this is happening? You don't want to overdo these questions but dropping them in at intervals (say at the halfway point in a one-hour meeting or before breaks in a longer process) is useful to surface tensions and anxiety that may be quietly building.

One nuance with questions is the distinction between how, what, and why. A lot of significant conversations are in search of "why." Yet simply using "why," particularly in the context of "Why did you ...," can sound accusatory or like an address to a misbehaving child. Questions using "how" and "what" can get you to the same place without that effect: What was the thinking behind___? How was that conclusion reached? What's going through your mind that___? How did that approach develop___?

Even the most skillful question in a conversation can start a *"Why is she/he/they asking that question?"* in the head of the other participant(s). This can invoke the Ladder of Inference and support the development of unhelpful stories. You can mitigate this by setting up your question with a grounding or explanatory statement, such as, *"I notice you're looking at your watch a lot. Is there somewhere else you need to be?"*

Physician leaders tend to operate in an environment where they and the people with whom they work are articulate, well educated, and often well read. It's been my experience that this contributes to a greater risk that rhetorical questions will creep into the significant conversation. Rhetorical questions aren't really questioning; they're a piece of theatrical artifice. They work well in monologues and presentations, so leave them there! They are "telling" dressed up as a question. If you feel the need to inject an idea into a conversation, just do it openly and honestly and own it. The format simply is *"I think that___ (insert what you want to say here)."*

Structuring a Conversation

There are ways of structuring an important conversation that help a leader avoid being led astray by their Ladder of Inference, falling foul of the Drama Triangle, keeping the conversation in the now, and making space to listen. The approach I describe here is taken from Gervase Bushe's Clear Leadership model and is referred to as the Experience Cube. It's a skill within the broader leadership framework of this model. There are some limitations looking at it in isolation, but it has appealing simplicity. You'll recall that the Ladder of Inference describes the largely unconscious generation of concepts as sensory input climbs through several cognitive- and emotional-filter layers. For example, you think you see a couple having an argument, but what you really see is a couple who are talking loudly, not smiling at each other, and using certain body language; you infer the argument as a result of what you think and feel about what you see and hear. In the Experience Cube, you slow the process of inference down somewhat and attempt to reflect on what you're experiencing at each level. It helps you to tell your experience and ask about everything else.

The Experience Cube has four components: Observations, Thoughts, Feelings, and Wants. The process starts with Observations: uninterpreted descriptions of what your senses tell you. This could be direct observations of events or behaviour, or verbatim recounting of what is reported to you. Language is very important here. In Rosalind's case, she can't say to Dr. Smith, *"You shouted at staff."* She can observe that *"I have received a complaint from human resources that you shouted at staff."* The first is an accusation; the second is something that can be shown to have happened. Just changing the sentence helps place her in a more neutral position in this sensitive matter.

The next component is "Thoughts." These are the impressions that form, the conclusions you draw, or the linkages you make to other issues. In Rosalind's conversation, for example, thoughts could include how the alleged behaviour would sit with the respectful workplace policy, whether this is something that is a pattern or unusual for Dr. Smith, or what process she thinks will be triggered by the events. When people say, *"This feels like___"* rather than *"I am feeling,"* they're using a simile or metaphor to express a thought, not a feeling.

Next, we move on to "Feelings." Feelings describe the emotions that are happening in the moment. Rosalind might feel apprehensive about doing this with a senior colleague. At the same time, she might feel worried that these reports are putting his position in jeopardy, or that the behaviour indicates that something isn't going well in his life. She may feel hostile if he comes in with that attitude. She may feel hurt if he verbally attacks her. She can choose to describe these feelings or not in the conversation, but things will go easier for her if she's aware of them. Describing feelings isn't the same as expressing feelings. We express feelings when they drive our behaviour. Describing our feelings is an effective strategy to prevent anger or resentment from taking over in a conversation.

Sometimes, acknowledging the feeling shifts the perspective and may take you back to re-examining thoughts and observations. Feelings come from our reptilian brain, which is in far closer contact with our actual sensory experience than our neocortex, where conscious thought lives. This subliminal recognition of a pattern of input gives rise to the *"something doesn't feel right"* intuitive experience. Any good, experienced physician will be able to give examples of times when this sense of vague anxiety, generated by a pattern in the incoming clinical data that didn't quite reach conscious awareness, averted a clinical disaster. Pay attention to it when it comes up in significant conversations. Stepping back into the conversation with *"I get the sense I may be missing something here. Can you tell me more about___"* can be a revealing strategy.

In this context, "Wants" (the final component) are the immediate wants that arise out of the interaction of Observations, Thoughts, and Feelings. While they should serve the overall purpose of the conversation, they're much more specific and immediate. In Rosalind's case, after her opening statement of the conversation, her want may simply be to hear Dr. Smith's version of events. His response generates new Observations, which in turn drive Thought, Feelings, and the *next* set of Wants.

Let's imagine that Rosalind is having her conversation with Dr. Smith in a room with a one-way mirror, and we're the audience behind the mirror. As the conversation proceeds, I will tag which of the techniques covered in this chapter are in play:

Rosalind has managed to find a time and place to meet with Dr. Smith. She did get some useful tips from Jim, who referred her to one of the hospital's organizational development specialists. The specialist worked with Rosalind to rehearse some techniques for this type of conversation. She's still apprehensive, but part of her is looking forward to trying out what she has learned in a real-life situation. She managed to book a small meeting room with a round table and a window looking out on the hospital's Remembrance Garden. There are usually four chairs at the table, but following a tip from an OD specialist, she gets to the room early and moves one against the wall and spaces three equally around the table. She then puts her bag on the chair with its back to the window, so that they won't be facing each other across a table. (Tribe—reducing physical barrier to group connection) Dr. Smith arrives.

"Good morning, Dr. Smith. Thank you for taking the time to meet with me. I know you have one of the busiest and most complex practices of all the psychiatrists here. (Rank) Is it still a good time for you?" (Autonomy— Process Question)

"As good as any, I suppose," he replies, frowning.

"Uh-oh," thinks Rosalind. But she takes a breath (managing the mirroring of hostility) and sails on. "As I said in our recent phone call, I've asked to meet with you concerning some complaints that have come to me via the Human Resources department. These complaints are concerning the way staff feel they've been treated. We're required, including all of us on the medical staff who are not employees (Tribe), both by our own policy, and now also by employment law, to follow that policy. We must look into such complaints at any level and find ways to resolve them. Employees have the right to insist that a third-party independent investigation be performed, but no one has gone that far yet. This means we have some breathing space to see if we can come to an understanding as to what was going on and informally find a way of helping everyone move past it. That's what I'm hoping to do today. (Bringing the conversation into now) As things stand,

we're not talking about doing anything to affect your practice or standing in the hospital. (Establishing the purpose of the conversation—Expectations) Is there anything you'd like to discuss in addition to this?" (Autonomy— Process Question)

Dr. Smith shrugs. "I think the whole thing is a lot of fuss about nothing, so ... no, I have nothing to add."

Rosalind continues. "Okay. The complaints refer to last Tuesday's and Thursday's Urgent Mental Healthcare clinics and were brought forward by the clinic manager. The complaint from the Tuesday clinic is that two nurses on separate occasions felt you were rude and dismissive when they asked for clarification of your orders. One reported to the manager that you said, loud enough for others to hear, 'What's wrong with you? Can't you read?' The other reported that, in a similar situation, you again loudly said, 'Isn't it obvious what I want? Do I have to explain every little detail?' On Thursday, the complaint is that one of the unit clerks noticed that your last patient hadn't arrived. When you finished with the previous patient, she came to tell you that she was trying to track them down. She complained that you yelled at her, saying, 'Are you trying to keep me here all day? If they're not here, they don't want to be seen. Who are you? Their mother?' The manager found her in tears later that afternoon. (Observation. Note that Rosalind is careful to say what the reports say, not to paraphrase in her own voice.)

"Human Resources feels, and I agree, that if these reports are accurate, that would be behaviour that violates our respectful workplace policy. (Thought) We're required to maintain a workplace free of that sort of stress for employees, or we face very severe penalties or fines. (Observation— Bringing the conversation into now) The manager, who has worked with you for a long time, was surprised and felt this was unusual for you (Observation—this was reported to Rosalind), and based on my interactions with you in the past, I would agree. (Thought) My first worry is that this sort of behaviour, if it's repeated, will lead to a formal complaint that could jeopardize your privileges, which would be bad for you but also for your colleagues who would have to deal with any impact on the service. I'm also worried as to whether something is wrong, that you're under some sort of stress that's influencing your behaviour. (Feelings) I really need to hear

what was happening those days from your perspective." (Want—Diagnostic Question—Sense Making)

"What's to understand? We don't seem to set any performance expectations of the staff these days, and sometimes doctors get frustrated with that. Instead of wasting my time, why aren't you on that manager to clean up her department's act?" (Confrontive Question—Dr. Smith clearly thinks she should be focussing her efforts elsewhere.)

Rosalind isn't getting through yet. "You're correct that the staff's performance is an accountability for that manager, and I'd say that respectful feedback to her about concerns with her staff's performance would be appropriate. (Thought) But that doesn't seem to be what's being described here. (Thought) We do have complaints (Observation), and we must follow a process to deal with them, as I have described. (Thought and reaffirming purpose of the conversation) If something comes out of the process that warrants attention, we can figure out the right way to go about it. (Thought— also creates an Expectation and serves Rank by implying that Dr. Smith's concerns are important, also Bringing the conversation into the now) I really need to get my head around what happened to generate those complaints, so let's look at this a bit more systematically. Tell me what was happening in those clinics on those days, just generally what was going on." (Want— Rosalind is now trying to get Dr. Smith to back up from his completed mental model about staff incompetence and just make Observations.)

Dr. Smith shrugs again. "It's an urgent care clinic. Patients are referred if they have urgent psychiatric issues that don't require emergency intervention. You can see anything. There was nothing special." (Thought, not observation—This is a judgement about the patient mix.)

"So, there was nothing that unusual or different that changed the stress level?" (Diagnostic Question—Emotions)

"No. And anyway, I've been doing this a long time. I'm not going to wilt because a patient gets a bit troublesome."

"I'm sure that's true. (Thought, Rank) If there was nothing else unusual going on that day, can you share any recollections of the encounters I just described?" (Diagnostic Question—Sense Making)

"Well, on the first day, I recall that there were a couple of instances when the nurse didn't seem to be bothering to read my orders." (Thought—This is a conclusion from the nurse's question, not an observation.)

"Can you tell me more about that?" (Diagnostic Question—Sense Making)

"What's to tell? I had to straighten them out!"

"So, what's involved in 'straightening out'?" (Diagnostic Question—Sense Making)

"I made it clear what I wanted and what I expected of them."

"How did that feel to you?" (Diagnostic Question—Emotions)

"What is this? Are you playing psychiatrist now? (Confrontive Question). Just because the hospital leadership has a fit of political correctness and appoints a ... young woman as Chief of Staff, doesn't mean you know what you're doing!"

Rosalind again takes breath and pauses. (Managing her emotional trigger in response to personal attack) "Dr. Smith, I'm aware almost every moment of how much more I need to know. I would love to have a conversation with you about my role and how you see I can best perform it at some point, but right now, we have the more pressing issue of making a satisfactory response to these complaints. (Reaffirming the purpose of the conversation) The complaints describe an emotional situation. The emotional experience of the complainants has been reported. In the spirit of fairness, I'm offering you the same opportunity. I'm curious. How were you feeling in those moments?" (Diagnostic Question—Emotions. Notice that, on the second attempt, Rosalind states her reason for the question and then asks the question.)

"I'm sure I was a bit frustrated. Who wouldn't be?" (Confrontive question)

Rosalind pauses for a moment, gathering her thoughts. "Let me summarize what I think I've heard so far. There was nothing particularly unusual happening that day, and you were frustrated by what you felt was subpar performance by the staff. (Observation) You told the staff of your frustration in a very direct way." Dr. Smith nods. Rosalind continues. "Where I'm struggling at this moment (Bring the conversation into now), Dr. Smith, is that you've been on the medical staff for over two decades, and there has never been a complaint about you like this before. (Observation) The clinic manager has worked with you for over five years, I think, and she has never seen this behaviour before. In all that time, I can't imagine that frustrations over staff interpreting orders, or *patients being late, hasn't happened before. (Thought) Yet these frustrations didn't generate this type of complaint in the past. If it wasn't the circumstance of the clinic that account for the change, and both you and the manager seem to agree on that, I must wonder if there's something changed about you. (Thought) Is there something else in play here?" (Diagnostic Question—Sense Making. This time, learning from her past misstep, Rosalind sets up the question with an explanatory statement first.)*

"Are you trying to pry into my personal life now?"

"I'm trying to understand why a senior and respected member of the medical staff (Rank) is the subject of concerning behavioural complaints. I'm getting the sense that I'm adding to your frustration with this process, and I feel sorry for that (Acknowledging the emotion and reinforcing her earlier explanation), but that doesn't change the role that's required of me here. (Reaffirming the purpose of the conversation.) The complaints describe behaviour that the hospital is required by law to sanction and keep out of its workplace. There are two ways of doing that. The first is to understand what's causing the behaviour and support the person in dealing with those causes. The second is to simply remove the person from the environment. (Thought) I would much prefer doing the first and would really regret the second. (Feeling) I've noticed that you haven't denied speaking to the staff in the way that was alleged. (Observation) What I think I'm hearing from you is justification for doing it. (Thought) My understanding of how this works is that you cannot justify this type of behaviour. You can, however, offer explanations that might help us choose a way to prevent it from happening again, as a way of avoiding severe repercussions. (Thought) I'm hoping you can tell me what the reasons are for what was happening for you that day. (Want) If I can offer no explanation for your behaviour, you're forcing the hospital to decide whether to risk this happening again or to simply remove you from the equation. (Thought) I have no authority to force you to tell me anything, but the less I know, the less I can help. I hate watching colleagues seem to struggle and not being able offer support. (Feeling) Is there anything you can tell me?" (Diagnostic Question—Sense Making)

Dr. Smith looks down and says nothing. A minute passes. Rosalind tries not to fidget and resists the urge to say something. Both Jim and the OD consultant had talked to her about the importance of silences in the conversation. She really needs a response from Dr. Smith now, and if she speaks first, she's letting him off the hook. He sighs and looks up.

"There is something. Last weekend was our thirtieth wedding anniversary." He pauses.

Rosalind finds all sorts of stories forming in her head. "Yes?" she says.

Dr. Smith seems to gather himself. "On the Monday, my wife got a phone call that her screening mammogram was abnormal. They asked her to come back urgently for a biopsy that Friday. We're still awaiting the results. Neither of us slept much last week, and to make matters worse, we had a big family party for the anniversary planned for Saturday, the day after the biopsy."

Rosalind was shocked. "I'm so sorry. I can't imagine what that must have felt like. (Rosalind is being empathic but not confusing, or fusing, her emotions with his.) How did your family take the news?" (Diagnostic Question— Sense Making)

"Well, we didn't tell them. Better not to worry them until we know what we're worried about."

"You're carrying this alone?" (Diagnostic Question—Emotions)

"Interesting phrase, 'carrying.' Quite perceptive—it does rather feel like a weight. Other than my wife's family doctor, I guess we are."

"I really hope it's not bad news. Now that you've raised this, do you think it's a factor in what we're discussing today?" (Diagnostic Question— Sense Making)

"It would be an understatement to say I've been preoccupied, yes. My family has always been blessed with good health, so we're learning about how to handle this as we go."

"Thank you for sharing it with me. I know what it's like to be a private person, and my sense is that telling me this wasn't easy for you. (Thought— Tribe) I do need to make a response to these complaints. (Want) I don't want to compromise your privacy at a difficult time, so do you have any suggestions on how I might communicate what we've discussed?" (Diagnostic Question—Actions)

Dr. Smith thought for a moment. "I can understand that saying nothing could put both of us in a difficult position. The wrinkle is that my daughter-in-law works in the hospital and knows several people in the clinic. If we say something to the staff before we've spoken to the family, that could be messy."

"Any thoughts on how we could get around that?" (Autonomy—inviting Dr. Smith to propose solutions first)

Dr. Smith sighed. "I'm beginning to think we have to tell our family. To be honest, my wife and I have been conflicted about that all along, with both of us taking both sides at different times. Is it possible to perhaps contain it in Human Resources for a day or two?" (Diagnostic Question—Actions)

Rosalind thinks for a moment. "How about we try this? I tell HR that there's a significant family issue, and you'd be willing to share some of the reasons more widely with the staff in a few days. In the interim, you acknowledge that your behaviour was not up to an appropriate standard, and you regret any harm that has resulted. We ask HR not to let it go any further until you and your wife have the biopsy results and you can be more definite about the plan. Would that work for now?" (Diagnostic Question—Actions)

"Yes. I think so. And I can count on your discretion, right?"

"You can to a point. You know I have a duty with respect to anyone whose health, state of mind, or actions might compromise patient care. I want to hear about what your plans are to look after yourself in this difficult time." (Want, Diagnostic Question—Actions)

Dr. Smith finally smiles. "Well, here's an irony. I do a fair bit of practice with referrals from the Physician Health program. If I were talking to me, I'd find a trusted colleague in whom I could confide and explore changing my schedule or taking leave until the crisis is past."

Rosalind is feeling very relieved where this is going now. "That sounds good, but there was an 'if' in there. Will you do it?" (Diagnostic Question—Actions)

Dr. Smith smiles again. "Maybe I've found a trusted colleague. I have to say you handled this better than I thought you would. But yes, I will follow my own advice."

"Thanks. I'll give you a call next week just to check in. I'm going to put together an email to HR, which I'll copy to you, saying we had this discussion. As to details, I'll just say that we have identified a significant family stress that contributed to the behaviour that caused concern. I'll say that I believe you now regret that behaviour, and we will be willing to release a bit

more information and explore next steps soon when things are clearer. And of course, I can say the behaviour will not be repeated, right?" (Rosalind has established what must happen after the conversation and created clarity on who is accountable for what.)

Dr. Smith sighs. "Yes, you can. I must apologize to you as well for causing you this trouble and for my earlier attitude."

"Thank you." says Rosalind. "This has been a good learning experience for me, and if there's anything I and the medical staff can do to help you, please don't hesitate to ask."

Did you note that Rosalind's approach was heavily based upon diagnostic questions? Did you notice that she used the word "I" frequently and "you" sparingly? Did you also notice that she didn't answer any of Dr. Smith's confrontive questions? Think of a recent significant conversation you've had and try to tease out the Observations, Thoughts, Feelings, and Wants that you experienced in that conversation and explore what sort of diagnostic questions you could ask to clarify your experience or extract that of the person with whom you're having the conversation. Try to use these techniques as often as you can; it takes practice! For a fuller appreciation of the context of these techniques, and to find other approaches that will support your communication skills, I strongly urge you to explore the references listed at the end of this chapter.

Key Learnings

- *Be aware that everyone experiences things differently and develop different mental models of the world.*

- *Know your own biases and support system measures to reduce the influence of prejudice and bias.*

- *For any important conversations, engage first, converse next.*

- *Select a time and place for important conversations that promote talking with rather than talking at.*

- *Frame the topic as something that is important to all parties, rather than framing it as a deficiency or accusation.*

- *Be ready for emotion, both yours and theirs.*

- *Keep the conversation in the present; the past cannot be changed; the future is fantasy.*

- *Inquire rather than state; use statements about your experience only to provide context to your questions about the other's experience.*

- *Be aware that what you intend and how it is received may be different; check in on how the other person understands what you are saying.*

FURTHER READING

Stories, Models, and Maps

Christopher Argryis, "Interventions for Improving Leadership-Effectiveness," *Journal of Management Development* 4 (1982): 30–51.

Trevor Maber, "Rethinking Thinking," July 1, 2021, https://ed.ted.com/lessons/rethinking-thinking-trevor-maber.

Jim Hicks and John McCracken, "The Dreaded Drama Triangle," *Physician Leadership Journal*, 1(2014): 62–65.

Lukas J. Volz and Michael S. Gazzaniga, "Interaction in Isolation: 50 Years of Insights from Split Brain Research," *Brain*, 140 (2017): 2015–2060.

Bias and Prejudice – The Dark Side of Mental Models

Nancy D. Spector, Philomena A. Asante, Jasmine R. Marcelin, Julie A. Poorman, Allison R. Larson, Arghavan Salles, Amy S. Oxentenko, and Julie K. Silver, "Women in Pediatrics: Progress, Barriers, and Opportunities for Equity, Diversity and Inclusion," *Pediatrics*, 144 (2019): https://pediatrics.aappublications.org/content/144/5/e20192149.

Amarette Filut, Madelyn Alvarez, and Molly Carnes, "Discrimination Towards Physicians of Colour: A Systematic Review," *Journal of the National Medical Association,* 112(2020): 117–140.

Oscar E. Dimant, Tiffany E. Cook, Richard E. Greene, and Asa E. Radix, "Experiences of Transgender and Gender Nonbinary Medical Students and Physicians," *Transgender Health*, 4.1 (2019): 209–216.

Project Implicit, "Implicit Association Test," July 1, 2021, https://implicit.harvard.edu/implicit/takeatest.html.

Setting the Stage

Kerry Patterson, Joseph Grenny, Ron McMillan, and Al Switzler, *Crucial Conversations. Tools for Talking When the Stakes Are High* (New York, NY: McGraw Hill, 2012).

Michael Bungay Stanier, "Three Habits to Have Your People with You not Against You," July 1, 2021, https://boxofcrayons.com/2015/07/three-habits-to-have-your-people-with-you-not-against-you/.

Ground Rules for the Conversation

Judith E. Glaser, *Conversational Intelligence. How Great Leaders Build Trust and Get Extraordinary Results* (New York, NY: Bibliomotion, 2014).

The Art of the Question

Edgar H. Schein and Peter A. Schein, *Humble Inquiry. The Gentle Art of Asking Instead of Telling* (Oakland, CA: Berrett-Koehler, 2021).

Michael Bungay Stanier, *The Coaching Habit. Say Less, Ask More & Change the Way You Lead Forever* (Toronto, ON: Box of Crayons Press, 2016).

Structuring the Conversation

Gervase R. Bushe, "Learning from Collective Experience," *OD Practitioner* 41(2009): 20–23

Gervase R. Bushe, *Clear Leadership. Sustaining Real Collaboration and Partnership at Work* (Boston, MA: Davies-Black, 2010).

OF COURSE, YOU REALIZE THIS MEANS WAR!

One Saturday morning, Sanjay is coming out of the supermarket, and he encounters Camilla, one of the cardiologists in his department. He asks her how things are going.

"Well," she replies, "the boys are misbehaving!"

Camilla, known for her sense of humour almost as soon as she arrived, refers to the two male colleagues in her division as "the boys." She is popular with the medical staff, and Sanjay has been impressed with her ability to see things clearly and problem solve.

"In what way?" he inquires.

"You know that we managed to get some increased staffing and another echocardiography machine, one that has more bells and whistles than our existing units? This means we can do some more complex and specialized examinations, although these are out of scope for techs and would need to be done by the docs. Alternatively, we do have a nasty waiting list for more routine exams. We could just bring this online and push the routine exams through with techs doing the exams and the docs reading."

"So, how is this making them behave badly?"

"When we first discussed it at a group meeting, we came up with those two scenarios, and the plan was that everyone would think about it, and we'd talk about it again in a couple of weeks. Then something happened. I'm not sure what, but the story I heard was that there was a chance encounter between the boys somewhere ... I think it was a kid's soccer match. One was leaning toward the specialized service, the other to killing the waiting list. Some things were said. I don't know what. But anyway, at the next meeting,

the one backing specialized services just launches straight in about some people not caring about providing best care but just wanting to make money by pushing through the numbers. The other retaliates by complaining that some people have no empathy for patients suffering and worrying while waiting for exams. They just want the glory of doing super-specialized, high-tech medicine that bills the big bucks. It went downhill from there. They're now communicating by sending messages through Annie (the other cardiologist) and I. It's like a bad TV sitcom!"

Sanjay is stunned. He had no idea this was happening. He'd always thought of this group as a happy bunch. "Do you want me to talk to them?"

Camilla thinks for a moment. "I appreciate the thought, but I'm a bit concerned that bringing in someone from outside the group, at least before we've had a crack at resolving this ourselves, might make them dig in even more. I wouldn't mind some help strategizing, though."

Sanjay smiles. "I'm pretty new to this too. Why don't I see if Chris, the Chief of Staff, has some time next week when she could talk to both of us? I'm pretty sure she's seen this sort of stuff before."

About Conflict

Science-fiction authors often dream up "Gaian" worlds in which all life lives in perfect harmony. The peace and quiet is never disturbed by clashes, violence, death, or destruction. That model has never really taken hold on Planet Earth. Our evolutionary history is defined by selection based on success in inter-species, intra-species, and species versus environment conflict. All the previous chapters have alluded to conflict in creating the need for the strategies each chapter promotes. Conflict is so enmeshed within human existence and human society that it has proven impossible to even create a single agreed-upon definition. It's part of the context of just about everything. If we think in evolutionary terms, there's only one reason why something could become so intertwined with our existence. We need it. It's possible that the internal experience of conflict keeps unresolved threats on our psychic agenda. Mastering conflict is about having tools to manage that agenda item and move on to the next one.

At this point, those of you who were hoping this chapter would show you the path to eliminating conflict are feeling a bit disappointed. As both a physician leader and coach, my experience is that fear of wading into conflict situations involving peers is one of the most common causes of physician reluctance to move to leadership. But take heart. We need to eat too, and while not everyone is a master chef, with a bit of patience and training, everyone can learn to boil an egg. So it is with conflict. The combination of some insight into your unconscious approach to conflict, some simple approaches to handling the structure of conflict, and employing some of the skills you've already seen in this book around engagement and conversations can enable you to manage most conflict. Certainly, some conflict needs expert intervention. But as a leader, you must believe that most conflict can be managed, and that your team and organization will be healthier for the conflict being out in the open. It happens to be true.

Let's sidestep the definition and consider the things that tell us that conflict is present. The first element is disagreement. That alone isn't enough, but if in that disagreement a negative emotional response is triggered, the internal experience of conflict is generated. The trigger is generally words or actions that assault our needs, our values, or our identity and internal image of who we are. Once triggered, this emotional response has an impact, and the Ladder of Inference is activated. We make assumptions that shape our beliefs about the person with whom we're in conflict. These beliefs change, usually for the worse. We selectively look for, or create, evidence that supports our story about them, which further fans the flames of our emotions, and the conflict escalates. It's been my experience that, in the world of high performing professionals, most conflict is triggered around values and identity. While assaults on physical needs are a primal cause of conflict and exist throughout the animal kingdom, I would suggest they are not common in the physician leadership world. There certainly can be arguments about share of resources, income, office space, access to Operating Room time, and other things that are justified as needs. But to claim physical needs as a cause for conflict implies that losing the conflict means you and your family will starve, not that you might have to settle for a smaller BMW. To qualify as needs, life, limb, or making a living at all must be on the line. Many "needs" based conflicts in the physician leadership landscape are about perceptions of unfairness (values), or perceptions of status (identity) that get paraphrased into stories of need to reinforce a victim role. That said, in the earlier chapter on motivation, I did introduce the idea that we need to achieve. Part of that, according to the tenets of self determination theory, is the need to increase our autonomy. Scratch the surface of many physician disputes, particularly those that are disputes between physicians and organizations, and you will uncover concerns about autonomy. This is something of a grey area as to whether this represents an issue of need or one of identity, but it can be an important conflict trigger, regardless of how it is categorized.

Where definitions of conflict have been attempted, they often talk about two or more parties engaging in some variety of mutually antagonistic behaviour. What is described above, which is how conflict starts in the human psyche, does not need two active participants. All of what is listed there happens in the mind of one person. The precipitating event and emotional trigger for a conflict may be something the conflicted person witnesses. Without a direct interaction with the person experiencing conflict, the antagonist(s) may be completely unaware of what they've started. The real importance of this is recognizing that the time that the conflict becomes visible is almost never the starting point. It's like a forest fire—undergrowth may smoulder for days before the flames erupt.

Mediator, author, and conflict coach Cinnie Noble includes the process described above as the first half of The (Not So) Merry Go Round of conflict. She refers to the point at which the internal experience of conflict becomes manifest externally as behaviour in a dispute as "the boundary." The boundary is an event or behaviour that creates the state in which reaction can be held back no longer. Unless they are party to the conflict, most leaders become aware of conflict in their groups or teams only when it crosses this boundary into open behaviour, and visible consequences occur. Once that point has occurred, life can truly become miserable. The conflict becomes the lens through which every issue, large or small, is viewed. Those at the edges sometimes withdraw in silence, a common behaviour among physicians. Physician leaders are often challenged to understand where the opinion of the majority lies when physicians choose silence over potentially being seen as critical or unsupportive of their warring colleagues. Sometimes, those on the sidelines are drawn in and pick a side. Sometimes this is because they too are triggered by the process, or because of the misinformation that often develops around conflicts. The saying "In war, truth is the first casualty" (Aeschylus 525–456 BC) can be applied much more widely than armed conflict. Often, the bystanders are drawn in by the need to belong and not separate from their peers. The anxiety about consequences of joining the fray is less than the perceived pain and risk of exclusion if one does not. These interactions generate more precipitating events, with more emotional triggers and yet more story making so that the cycle of conflict is maintained, and often intensified.

You will notice almost all the foregoing discussion is about emotion. As I alluded to in the chapter on significant conversations, once conflict is established, the "facts" play an exceedingly small role. The experiences of those involved (the so called "facts") that led to the conflict are now in the past. Everyone's version of them is immutable, but also everyone's version is usually different! Trying to manage conflict by arguing about the past is futile, yet it consumes huge amounts of time and energy. Conflict consultant Liane Davey has a great saying: "Facts don't fix fights." It's true. Their main and perhaps only value are as vehicles to understand what triggered a disagreement into conflict. Conflict management is about managing emotion in the present and designing actions in the future, not rewriting the past. This chapter will outline some approaches, which are covered in more detail in the "Further Reading" references. But first let us look at ...

Knowing Your Own Conflict Preference

Efforts to understand and better manage workplace conflict outside of medicine have quite a long history, with publications dating back sixty years or more. One model that has persisted is that developed by Kenneth Thomas and Ralph Kilmann. This model classifies preferred conflict style along two axes: assertiveness and cooperativeness (Figure 6). The resulting styles are

Avoiding, Competing, Accommodating, Collaborating, and Compromising. Those who prefer avoiding will sidestep conflict and are content with a situation in which no one's needs are met. Accommodating refers to complying with the wants of the other party without regard for your own. These preferences are quite common, perhaps because as children we were often encouraged to "not make trouble." Finding ourselves in conflict with siblings and peers was one step away from finding ourselves in trouble with parents and teachers. Competing is the reverse; you attempt to secure your wants without regard to the other party's. Collaborating is a process that attempts to obtain a result that meets the most needs of all parties. Compromising occurs when the situation is managed by incompletely meeting the wants or needs of all the parties. This type preference can be measured with a validated instrument using thirty choice pairs, the Thomas-Kilmann Conflict Mode Instrument. This is now an online assessment that anyone can take; the link is in the "Further Reading" section. Knowing your preference on this spectrum tells you where your natural inclination in responding to conflict lies. It doesn't tell you the approaches of which you are capable. Neither does it tell you which approaches are correct. Sometimes, conflicts are "Not the hill to die on!" In these cases, Avoiding or Accommodating may be wise strategies. A petty squabble over a parking spot, or which clinic room somebody uses, may fall into this category. A decision to sidestep the conflict or merely cave to the wishes of another party should be made carefully, however. Liane Davey has introduced a useful concept to consider in these situations: the notion of conflict debt. She defines this as "the sum of all contentious issues that need to be addressed to move forward but instead remain undiscussed and unresolved."[2]

Any avoided or accommodated conflict will generate some conflict debt. Are you contributing to a perception that someone is favoured over others? Are you supporting a narrative that you're unwilling to deal with tough issues? Are you rewarding an existing pattern of bad behaviour? It may well be that the price is worth the value gained in not fighting this battle, but that needs to be a rational rather than an emotional decision. Sometimes conflict arises over something where there is an absolute

2 Liane Davey, *The Good Fight. Use Productive Conflict to Get Your Team and Organization Back on Track* (Canada: Raincoast Books,1929): 10.

standard. For example, imagine a conflict with a surgeon who refuses to use the preoperative checklist. This is a situation where his interest cannot be accommodated at the expense of patient safety, at least if he wishes to continue operating. Competing is the best approach.

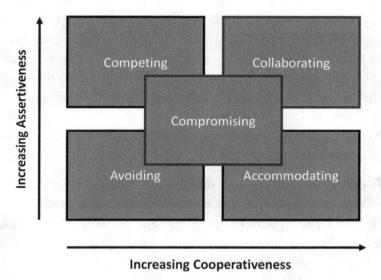

Figure 6. *The Thomas-Kilmann Conflict Style Model.*

Sometimes, situations are such that the only way forward involves some shared misery. Compromising is the path. This may be a good starting point when resource limitations are imposed across programs that must keep operating. Simply ending one or more of them is not tenable. Where all interests in a conflict have some merit and are potentially attainable, Collaborating is worth a try. In Sanjay's situation, described at the beginning of this chapter, reducing wait lists and offering more specialized services both seem reasonable goals. Exploring whether, in time, both might be possible is a reasonable approach.

No one has all these style preferences, but knowing your preference will help you understand the level of effort and support required to use the most appropriate approach. The further the approach is from your natural place on the grid, the more support you might need to practise that style.

Conflict and Psychological Safety

As a conflict coach, I find that psychological safety is now invariably brought up in physician conflicts in which I'm asked to assist. It may seem a bit odd introducing it in a chapter on conflict, but it has been my experience that conflict is often what stimulates discussions about psychological safety. Sometimes these are genuine exploratory conversations to get to a better work environment. Starting the conversation during conflict, however, often results with the term becoming weaponized. The words and actions of parties in a dispute are framed by other parties as part of a story of absent psychological safety. The discussion of what is lacking almost always occurs in the absence of any discussion of what is needed.

Psychological safety is emphatically *not* the absence of conflict. Quite the reverse. Psychologically safe environments wear their conflict openly. They separate issues from people and move on. Timothy Clark, whose consulting company, LeaderFactor, does a lot of work in this area, has a useful definition of a psychologically safe environment as one of "rewarded vulnerability." He further identifies the areas of vulnerability to be rewarded as inclusion, learning, contribution, and challenge. Inclusion safety means accepting people for who they are as people, being sensitive to human attributes, feelings, and demographics. Learning safety implies an environment where people can be comfortable acknowledging their limits and seeking support to enhance their abilities. Contribution safety means environments where people can demonstrate competence and expect appreciation and constructive and useful feedback. They can also expect to gain autonomy as they demonstrate mastery. Challenge safety means being able to express ideas that may be contrary to the existing practice or direction. It also means expecting to have a fair hearing of those ideas, without negative consequences. It doesn't mean those ideas will be accepted.

Clark goes to great pains to reinforce that psychological safety is not gratuitous niceness. It's not a licence to be unaccountable to role expectations or contract deliverables, and it's not an expectation that decision making in hierarchical organizations is going to be democratized and shared. It's not an expectation that people will be protected from the consequences of their actions or that they can keep their jobs or roles no matter what. It's not about being politically correct. It's possible to respect human attributes and culture and still have accountability. A full discussion of developing these types of safety is beyond the scope of this book, but you'll find the references in the "Further Reading" section helpful in implementing psychologically safer practices.

If we perceive an environment as unsafe, it usually means we fear something in that environment. Fearing consequences doesn't always mean an environment is psychologically unsafe. Let's imagine a physician who is employed under contract to provide certain clinical services. Compared to his or her peers in the same environment, he or she is underdelivering. The leader is required to make them aware that, if they continue to underdeliver, their contract will not be renewed. What determines whether this environment is psychologically safe or not is how this situation unfolds. The leader could check in at regular intervals, creating awareness of the issue early and setting clear expectations. They could provide appropriate learning and skill-development opportunities to rectify the deficit. They could identify and provide appropriate support for any health or out of work issues that are affecting performance. If all that fails, they could consider a supportive exit strategy if the person cannot meet the demands of the role. The person could still lose their job, but nothing in that process would be considered psychologically unsafe. On the other hand, if the leader doesn't particularly like this person, they might be unclear in expectations, let the performance deficits pile up, and then just announce at the minimum-notice interval that the contract will not be renewed. Once the word gets around that this is the way things are done around here, you will have a well-established psychologically unsafe environment.

Leaders are often held accountable for psychological safety in their areas. That doesn't mean that leaders are the only ones whose behaviour can compromise psychological safety. Psychologically unsafe environments don't call out gossiping about others. They allow inflammatory emails, particularly using "reply to all." They don't welcome and support newcomers—worse, they treat them with suspicion, tricks, and traps. They may have well-established factions and cliques. They support, or at least permit, stories that some groups are more important or more valuable than others. Individuals or groups engage in deception and one-upmanship to get resources. It's not unusual for bad environments to have poor leadership, but one should be cautious about assigning cause and effect. Leaders are an important factor in workplace culture, but they're not the only factor. It takes strong and courageous leadership to turn around a toxic workplace culture. It's not surprising that competent leaders may hesitate before jumping into the fire, leaving the field clear for less promising candidates. These candidates often come from within the toxic culture they help create and maintain.

Conflict and Shame

Shame is what happens when we are confronted within our own minds with an image of ourselves that we don't like. It's a shortcut to strong negative emotions when we confront the perception that we aren't the ideal person we aspire to be. Physicians are really good at shame. The intense academic competition to get into medicine selects for individuals who have been academically strong or outstanding all their lives. These individuals often develop an unachievable self image of unfailing perfection, in part by themselves but often with the help of well-meaning teachers and family. Sometimes individuals are caught in family medical tradition and suppress their own non-medical ambitions to comply. They live in conflict every day they work. Having selected shame-sensitive individuals to populate medicine, many are trained, even now, in systems that use shaming as a pedagogical tool. While awareness of this dark side of medicine is increasing, evidence is strong that the lack of learning safety, as Timothy Clark would put it, remains pervasive in medical culture. It's been shown to exist in student, resident, and medical-faculty interactions, between and amongst all the levels. In the clinical environment, it has been found in intra- and interdisciplinary teams and is recognized as a major barrier to positive quality improvement culture.

It's no surprise that physician leaders, when dealing with conflict, see shame frequently used as a weapon. Physicians in dispute will comb the archives for examples of their colleagues', leaders', or organization's failings to diminish their opponents with shame. Not surprisingly, issues arising that may cast a negative light on a physician or physician group's performance or behaviour have a high probability of touching a shame button. Physicians have woven their professional competence deeply into their identity or self image. This brings the possibility of shame from tarnishing that image close to the surface. As a result, physicians' responses in conflict situations often align with predicted patterns in response to shame. Author and researcher Brené Brown identifies a long list of workplace behaviours that are associated with shame. A number that are commonly seen in the landscape of physician leaders, particularly in conflict, include:

- **Perfectionism** - Individuals not only hold themselves to high standards but very publicly do so to others as well. If found to be less than perfect, they will argue that they are perfect in the face of evidence to the contrary, a behaviour known as competence compulsion.

- **Gossiping** - Going to great pains to make sure that the stories circulating about the other folks are worse than ones circulating about you.

- **Back-channeling** - Physicians or other, usually senior, healthcare professionals use their connections and social status or networks to erode the reputation of those with whom they are in conflict

- **Power over** - This overlaps with back-channeling and often involves the use of the veiled threat. "I know X (person of power or authority), so you might want to be careful if you don't want them finding out." This one is particularly powerful as a noxious influence in the world of residents and students, who fear bad or mediocre references will kill their career aspirations.

- **Withdrawal** - Individuals refuse to participate or engage at the minimum level possible.

- **Blaming** - The fault lies with others, commonly the organization.

- **Weaponized humour** - Self-deprecating humour in moderation is not a bad thing to reduce interpersonal tension. As well-educated and often very articulate individuals, physicians can be deadly at using humour and sarcasm to shame, humiliate, or embarrass.

All these behaviours are very effective at driving a cycle of conflict. A physician leader dealing with conflict needs to recognize them and call them out.

Rather than manage the shame behaviours, every effort should be made to keep shame off the agenda. The most important skill in this has already been covered in the chapter on significant conversations. It's the skill of framing the topic. Whether you, as a leader, are in conflict, or you are intervening in a conflict, creating a starting point that focuses on the issue and not the person is vital. In Sanjay's example, he and Camilla could approach this by saying, *"We are going to figure out which of you is right about the new echo machine."* That probably will not end well. Or they could say, *"Let's have a conversation about the possibilities the new echo machine creates."*

The next helpful strategy is to block any conversation other than people describing their own experience. This means calling out hearsay or quoting others who are not present to speak for themselves. It means calling out speculation about other people's thoughts and motives. It means prohibiting commentary on actions, events, or behaviours that were not witnessed. It's quite amazing how quickly the temperature of conversation lowers when those items, all of which are mental constructs or stories, are taken out of the equation. These prohibitions also eliminate almost all intentional shaming strategies. Things may still be said that generate shame, but shame coming from hearing the effect one's action had on someone else is a quite different process than being shamed intentionally by an attack on ourselves. Recognition of genuinely shameful actions is a step toward accepting vulnerability, a necessary precursor to developing trust in any relationship.

Conflict Management Techniques

The availability of professionals who are trained to intervene and manage conflict has certainly increased in recent years. Given that conflict is a part of any human environment, outsourcing its management in all or most cases could be very time consuming and expensive. Very few conflicts require external intervention. Many of those only reached that point because the opportunity for thoughtful people of good intention to use simple and early interventions was missed.

As mentioned in the previous section, the simple act of not ignoring a conflict is a highly effective step. Using the conversation techniques described in the previous chapter to engage the individuals or groups in conflict, having them describe how things are landing for them and express their desires will probably allow forward movement on a large proportion of conflicts. Common sense still has much to recommend it. If the emotional temperature of a conflict can be lowered sufficiently so that activation of fight or flight responses is calmed and higher cognitive processing restored, common sense can often prevail. Not acting when you see conflict, however, allows the conflict to go through multiple cycles and develop ever more layers of negative emotion and misleading stories.

Using a structure like the Ladder of Inference to truly explore a conflict is both a powerful personal insight and a good technique for a leader to understand what is behind a situation when it comes to their attention. Rather than spend of a lot of time on the polished story of the conflict, try working through it in steps. like rungs on the Ladder:

1. *When did you first get the feeling you were in a conflict on this* (what was the base data that started this process)*?*

---

2. *Why did this trigger a negative emotional reaction for you? Did it offend one or more of your basic needs, cherished values, or your identity* (which data did you select)?

_____

3. *What was the impact of this on you? Did it make you feel shamed* (what meaning did you assign to this)?

_____

4. *What assumptions did you make about the actions (what they did), the intentions (what they were trying to do), and the motivations (why they were trying to do it) of the other party* (what are the assumptions in your model of what happened)?

_____

5. *What do you now believe about the other party in the conflict* (what are your beliefs)?

_____

6. *What did you then do* (what actions resulted from your beliefs)?

_____

This approach is part of the CINERGY conflict coaching framework, but it's one that coaches encourage clients to learn and practise as an ongoing conflict management skill. There are several ways of using this approach, including doing it with both parties. It can be done with one party, who then imagine themselves as the other party and try to answer the questions from the other perspective. It will invariably demonstrate that the conflict is being largely driven by assumption and belief. These beliefs then create the behaviours that fuel the cycle of conflict. It creates an excellent opportunity to invite people to look at the situation based on "what if" their assumptions were replaced by different ones. Question 6 can then be replaced with, *"If that were true, what would you like to do?"* Note that while the approach establishes the connection between the precipitating event and the emotional response, it doesn't seek to dispute or change them. How someone has experienced an event in the past is what it is; it is now beyond change.

Recognizing a trigger point for conflict, however small, creates the opportunity for early intervention. Such a strategy was proposed by John Sherwood and John Glidewell in 1972, called "Pinch theory" (Figure 7). Their model of conflict proposes that we frequently experience several minor triggers, or "pinches," over time in a relationship. We tend to ignore, or at least not react externally, to these small provocations. At some point, though, the pressure to react becomes too much. We then have a "crunch" where the conflict surfaces to our overt behaviour. We then either withdraw without any resolution but much ill-feeling, triangulate by expressing our frustrations to others, which makes us feel better but does nothing the help the issue, or enter a challenging negotiation to try to restore the relationship. The strategy proposed here is to have a planned discussion as soon as there is a pinch, to "nip it in the bud." This concept has been adopted by several other communication and conflict models. Applying the techniques that are covered in the chapters on engagement and significant conversations will serve you well here.

Liane Davey has proposed several "Conflict Strategies for Nice People." While all have merit, I'd like to highlight three: Two Truths, Question the Impact, and Common Criteria, which I believe can be particularly effectively applied by physician leaders. Two Truths requires that parties to the conflict validate each other's perspective. Get them to repeat the other's position, asking clarifying questions as they need to. It's not unusual for them to find ways to strengthen the other's case. The conversation is framed as both proposals being meritorious or true. When using this approach, make it tactile. Have the parties write down their summary of each other's position on flip charts or either side of a white board. The challenge is now a shared one of finding a way to make both happen. This concept frames one of the oldest physician conflicts in organized healthcare: the duty of physicians to advocate for the

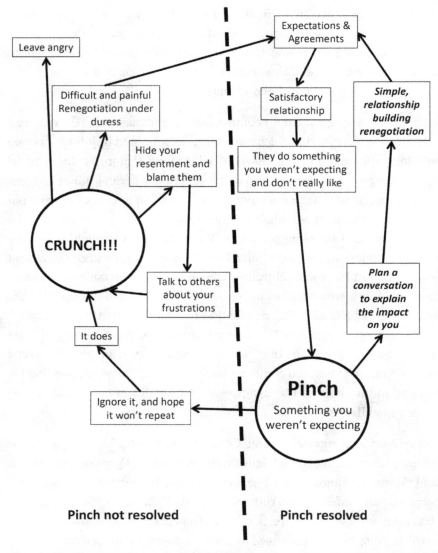

Figure 7. Sherwood and Glidewell's Pinch Model of Dealing with Conflict (adapted from John J. Sherwood and John C. Glidewell," in W. W. Burke (ed.) Contemporary Organization Development *[1972])*

needs of individual patients versus the duty of the system to provide the best care to the most people.

The Two Truths opens the door to another enormously powerful approach to problem solving and decision making: integrative thinking. This approach, championed by Jennifer Riel and Roger Martin from the Rotman School of Management at the University of Toronto, encourages taking different proposals in a conflict or problem and deconstructing the mental models behind them back down the Ladder of Inference to create alternatives that capture the essential elements of each. Imagine your parties are standing in front of their white board with their summaries of their positions. They could start by asking each other what the beliefs are that created their position, then the assumptions, then the data selected, and then what data was available. With that all information in hand, inquiries into other possibilities and discussions that kick the tires of novel approaches are enabled. There are, of course, many other aspects and nuances to this approach, but I'd encourage you to explore the reference to this in the "Further Reading" section.

"Question the Impact" is a good approach when a party to a conflict has real concerns about something that is being presented by the other side. In the heat of the moment, this commonly is expressed as an attack on the character or competence of the other party. This is an example of the attacking party's behaviour being ruled by a story about the other's character or competence, rather than by curiosity about the other's thinking. On the other hand, responding with *"I think I understand what you're saying, but I have some concerns. How would you see this working with___"* or *"What would the effect on X be?"* Keep asking "how" or "what" questions until either the fears are allayed, or the other party finds a way of adjusting their idea to fit the new dimensions brought in by the questions. This approach encourages the demonstration of competence rather than attacking it.

Common Criteria is a good approach for complex and nuanced situations. This is another good one for white boards and flip charts. Get the parties to list all the issues that need to be addressed and then discuss priorities. The point here is to create a situation where all parties feel the content reflects what has brought them into conflict. This can also work into an integrative thinking approach to novel solutions as you drill down into the thinking behind each listed issue. This process is helpful at teasing out mutual or complementary interests around which negotiation, to be discussed in the next section, can occur.

Negotiation and Conflict

Conflict, negotiation, mediation, and arbitration are words that commonly crop up together. Negotiation can play an important role in moving forward in conflict, but it also has some limitations. Negotiation and its specialized partners, mediation and arbitration, are particularly good at dealing with specific issues. Negotiation by itself has much less effect on the emotional landscape. So far in this chapter, I've emphasized conflict as an emotional experience. The strategies suggested so far are ones in which the physician leader helps manage the emotions in play. Sometimes the emotional trigger(s) is a specific issue that invites a specific solution. Often, however, it's a pattern of incidents that have kept fuelling the emotions of conflict. Where things get confusing is when emotionally based conflicts find specific issues around which to build stories that justify the conflict. Where people just detest each other, negotiation is at best a holding strategy until the next flare up.

Arguably the most popular reference in negotiation is *Getting to Yes*, by the late Roger Fisher, William Ury, and Bruce Patton, which has sold millions of copies and is still in press after forty years from the first edition. While it provides many practical tips on negotiation, there are a couple worth highlighting for combination with the other techniques of engagement and significant conversation that I have already introduced. The first is to focus on interests, not people. This aligns with the concept of framing significant conversations in ways that don't push buttons. It also reduces the risk of triggering a shame response. For example, "We need to have a look at the way the call schedule is working out, particularly the way long weekends are falling. I'd like to be sure that, over one or two years, they are being distributed more or less equally across the group."

This statement identifies an issue, the distribution of holiday call, and establishes an interest, the person wants an equal spread.

Imagine how this alternate opening would land: "You're always sneaking in call requests that get you out of long weekends!" Good luck with that negotiation. If everyone can agree that having equal share of the long weekends on call is a good idea, there's a mutual interest around which to negotiate. But what if a member of the group pipes up and says, "I've signed up to do an online master's degree. I need some extra time off during the week and can't take call on Wednesdays due to online classes." This person now has introduced a new interest that does not conflict with the original. If this person is willing to trade protection from being on call or post call on their class days, freeing up some clinic time for study, maybe they can cover a few more holidays and relieve the burden for the rest of the group. As such, their interest is complementary and can support negotiation. Interests exist in the moment as part of someone's experience.

The other particularly important concept that comes out of *Getting to Yes* is the "Best Alternative to a Negotiated Agreement," or BATNA. This means having a plan, in advance of the negotiation, as to what you will do if you're unable to negotiate a solution. Many conflicts fester for lack of this. The most common example I see is a small-unit or middle-level physician leader confronting someone about unacceptable performance or behaviour. They're unable to secure tangible and trackable commitment to change. But they enter the negotiation around a behavioural undertaking without planning to take the alternate step to escalate the behaviour to senior leadership, where the adverse consequences will be greater, if their negotiation fails. Instead, they throw up their hands, say, "Don't do it again," and hope. As the famous quotation says, hope is not a strategy. Another common example is imagine you are unhappy about working conditions or payment, and may be seeking to better both. You may make empty threats to quit if you don't get what you want. If this done with with no preparation, it can easily backfire. On the other hand, quietly exploring serious options for career alternatives, and coming to the table able to show, or even just being aware yourself that you have real options, is a different matter. At an emotional level, knowing you have at least one other option reduces your level of flight or flight response. Having that one degree of autonomy may enhance your ability to engage with the other party and move toward success at the emotional level.

Mediation is a term that often comes up in conflict. Mediators are very skilled people who work with all parties in a dispute to achieve agreement. Like negotiation, it tends to be about an issue or issues that are tangible enough to create some specific agreement. Mediators usually work with individual parties to understand their experience; then they work between the parties to lay the groundwork for options, and then work with the parties present. As a conflict coach, the most common way that a situation is presented to me is "We would like you to mediate between___." After explaining that I'm not a mediator, I then explore whether this is about people not getting along to the point that psychological and patient safety are compromised, or whether there's a specific issue to be resolved. If the former, coaching may be worth a try; if the latter, mediation may be the correct route. Conflict coaching uses coaching inquiry techniques to develop insight and new perspectives on conflict, and support the choice and design of action to move through conflict. It can take the form of coaching a leader to manage conflict in their team, a useful pre-emptive strategy. It can also support one, some or all parties in a conflict. Conflict coaching does not presume a specific solution; that is for the parties being coached to decide. It is the strategy of choice where emotional issues are the dominant feature of the conflict. It is not mutually exclusive from negotiation, mediation or arbitration, and commonly precedes or occurs in parallel with them in complex situations. Helping get emotional behaviour under control can dramatically increase the value of issues based approaches.

Physician leaders often need to be part coach, part mediator. Arbitration is slightly different in that a third party will decide the outcome based upon what the parties to the conflict submit to the process. This can be a reasonable position for a leader to take, for example, on a time-sensitive issue. Imagine you have two groups who are holding up the implementation of a mandated surgery program because they cannot agree. The physician leader might say, "We can't wait any longer on this. You have until

Friday to solve this. If you can't, I'll review any ideas you put forward, but I'll make a decision no later than next Wednesday on how the program will be implemented." This is the physician leader as arbitrator.

Let's see how Sanjay and Camilla are doing:

Sanjay and Camilla bump into each other again about a month later, having lunch on the hospital lawns on a sunny day. They had met with Chris for nearly two hours a few days after their initial conversation. Sanjay knows there have been two or three group meetings since, but he hasn't heard anything and is hoping no news is good news. He asks her how it's going.

Camilla smiles. "Remarkably well, actually. Annie and I took Chris's advice and first told them how their behaviour was landing on us, and we made it clear that we weren't going to play. If they wanted to keep behaving the way they were, they'd be talking to you and Chris about it. Annie took one of the boys, and I took the other, and we got them to tell us what was going on. It seems that they've been annoying each other in little ways for some time but never said anything. When the daughter of one accidentally fouled the daughter of the other at a soccer match (I won't tell you which, to protect the innocent) and it wasn't called, that just lit the blue touch paper and off they went.

"We then had a meeting in which we just talked about what they were doing to annoy each other. It was a bit awkward, but it went okay. One of the things that came up for both boys was that they're as good as each other at jumping to conclusions. We agreed we did need to talk about how to get the best value out of the new echo machine and the extra staffing, but at the first meeting, we got everyone to promise that they weren't allowed to propose anything until there was data to back it up. I then took Chris's suggestion to connect with the process engineer they hired in quality improvement. He looked at our clinic numbers. In no time, he was able to identify the number of exams we need to do to bring the waiting list down, and the ongoing number of extras we need to do to stop it from going up again. The second number was surprisingly small. It turns out we've been quietly falling behind for a long time. We then had another meeting, where instead of arguing about what to use the machines for, we discussed the timing of using the resources initially to kill the backlog while we try out the new

exams. As the backlog comes down, we'll start transitioning in more of the specialized exams. It turns out that, once we catch up, we only need to use that station for regular exams three mornings per week, and everyone can live with that."

Sanjay is impressed. "Wow, that is quite a result. Great job! Maybe you should be doing my job."

Camilla chuckles. "One day, perhaps when you're sick of it. But you did your job; you got me what I needed. You're entitled to pat yourself on the back."

Key Learnings

- *Recognize that conflict is a normal part of human relationships.*

- *Be aware of your own preferred conflict style; practice or find support to work in other styles where they are more appropriate.*

- *Do not try to create psychological safety by avoiding or suppressing conflict; work to surface and work through conflict constructively instead.*

- *Understand your shame triggers and those with whom you work. Be sensitive to shame behaviours as a source of conflict.*

- *Act sooner in conflict rather than later; do not let small issues become large ones.*

- *Use good conversation techniques to share and understand individual experiences in a conflict; this is often enough to resolve most interpersonal conflicts.*

- *If you cannot work through a conflict that is impacting you or your work, seek skilled help rather than give up.*

- *Where conflict involves a specific issue external to people's feelings about each other, consider mediation or arbitration.*

FURTHER READING

About Conflict

Cinnie Noble, *Conflict Management Coaching. The Cinergy Model* (Toronto, ON: CINERGY Coaching, 2012).

Liane Davey, *The Good Fight. Use Productive Conflict to Get Your Team and Organization Back on Track* (Richmond, BC: Raincoast Books, 2019).

Knowing Your Own Conflict Preference

Kenneth W. Thomas and Ralph H. Kilmann, "The Thomas-Kilmann Conflict Mode Instrument," July 1, 2021, https://kilmanndiagnostics.com/overview-thomas-kilmann-conflict-mode-instrument-tki/.

Conflict and Psychological Safety

Timothy R. Clark, *The 4 Stages of Psychological Safety. Defining the Path to Inclusion and Innovation* (Oakland, CA: Berrett-Koehler, 2021).

Timothy R. Clark, "The Hazards of a 'Nice' Company Culture," *Harvard Business Review,* June 20, 2021, https://hbr.org/2021/06/the-hazards-of-a-nice-company-culture.

Conflict and Shame

Jennifer J. Robertson and Brit Long, "Medicine's Shame Problem," *Journal of Emergency Medicine,* 57(2019): 329–338.

Brené Brown, *dare to lead* (New York: Random House, 2018).

Conflict Management Techniques

John J. Sherwood and John C. Glidewell, "Planned renegotiation: a norm-setting OD intervention." in W. W. Burke (ed.) *Contemporary Organization Development* (Durham, NC: NTL Institute, 1972): 35–46.

Mark Horstman, "The Pinch Crunch Model," *Manager Tools,* July 15, 2021, https://www.youtube.com/watch?v=BPmb-bebnks.

Liane Davey, *The Good Fight. Use Productive Conflict to Get Your Team and Organization Back on Track* (Richmond, BC: Raincoast Books, 2019).

Jennifer Riel and Robert L. Martin, *Creating Great Choices* (Boston MA: Harvard Business School Publishing, 2017).

Negotiation and Conflict

Roger Fisher, William Ury, and Bruce Patton, *Getting to Yes: Negotiating Agreement Without Giving In* (New York, NY: Penguin, 2011).

IF THERE IS NO "I" IN TEAM, WHAT AM I DOING HERE?

Susan is a bit surprised to hear the front door close a bit harder than seems necessary. Rosalind comes into the kitchen and flops her backpack on the table. "Aaargh ... people!" is all she says.

Susan raises an eyebrow. "Could you be a little more specific?"

"It's that working group to reform the Medical Advisory Committee— again. We had our first meeting six weeks ago, and everything seemed fine and clear. We had another one about three weeks ago, which wasn't as great, as we seemed to be covering a lot of the same ground as the first one. But today, today was just ... I don't know ... like everybody had forgotten why we were there and like they'd all come to the meeting with a hangover!"

"It seems hard to believe that they're all misbehaving."

"Well, one or two are being pretty difficult at times. The other four sort of politely look the other way when that happens. But even with them, I'll say something and then ... then there will be either be no response or some oblique comment to the effect of wondering if there's another agenda in play. Not that they'll just come out and say what's on their minds. There was nothing like this when we first proposed the idea."

Susan thinks for a moment. "I remember a session we did when I was going for my level 2 coaching. I think I still have the notes. It was about the different stages groups of people go through when they're pulled together as teams or similar groups." Susan had been a high-level volleyball player and still volunteered as a coach at the high school and sometimes university level.

This time Rosalind raises an eyebrow. "A group of high-powered physicians is hardly the same as a gaggle of sweaty teenagers!"

Susan chuckles. "You're right—they could hardly be worse. But my recollection was that this has been validated in many settings. What I remember is that we were told that this sort of friction was normal, and that it was important to work through it to get the group to bind together and start working as a team. Let's play with Google; I'm sure it can't be hard to find."

The Natural History of Teams

The concept of teamwork being essential to healthcare is one of the most common statements that healthcare leaders make. The ability to form and manage effective teams may be the most important function of healthcare leadership. Despite this, examples of team dynamics and team leadership skills being introduced into medical training aren't easy to find, although awareness in nursing education and literature has been growing for some time. Teams are special. While people naturally aggregate into groups based on some shared interest or characteristic, teams are more complex. Members of teams share a common purpose, and the achievement of that purpose requires that they depend on each other for success. The goal can be achieved by the team but not by the individuals in the team acting independently. When a team comes together, it's useful to think about it as a new collective lifeform. Like all living things, teams have a usual pattern of development and do not spring fully formed and functional into existence. Successful team leadership requires understanding and working with the natural developmental trajectory of teams.

The most widely quoted model of team development was first published by Bruce Tuckman in 1965. It initially had four elements: Forming, Storming, Norming, and Performing. In a review of publications on human group behaviour under different circumstances (group therapy, training groups, natural groups, and laboratory study groups), he noted authors described a common sequence of behaviours that he characterized with these terms. In 1977, a fifth element, Adjourning, was added.

There are other more complex models, but the theme of initial conditional engagement, passage through difficulties, interpersonal conflict and doubt, and developing confidence preceding ultimate performance is seen in all. There are also many models of team effectiveness. These focus more on the behaviours and external conditions that contribute to team success rather than developmental trajectory. Tuckman's basic observations and the inferences they generate for leadership behaviour, however, cover most of what a physician leader needs to understand to have a basic competence in working with teams.

While the four initial stages of the Tuckman model are widely published, some of the more detailed nuances are less well known but are also useful. Tuckman further subdivided each stage into Group Structure and Task Activity. The former characterizes the behaviour and feelings of the team members towards each other at each stage. The latter describes feelings and behaviour towards the team's task.

Leading a Forming Team: Defining Tasks and Roles

The forming team often gives the impression of excitement and potential. Unless the team is some sort of externally forced marriage of individuals to a task, people are there to get something done that aligns with their self-determination needs. It will allow them to demonstrate competence, will develop or reinforce relationships, and they will gain in status and autonomy. At the same time, however, they are in a new social setting. The neurophysiological processes that determine their level of engagement are in play. They are looking for evidence of group or subgroup connection with the team. They are seeking clarity and certainty about the purpose of the team and their role in it. They are comparing and testing themselves against other members to understand the status hierarchy. They are wondering how much control they have. Outward behaviour in the forming phase tends to be polite. Overt conflict is unusual unless it was pre-existing. At this stage, any activity around the task tends to be about achieving clarity on the nature of the task. This is also the time that the differentiation of roles within the team begins. As such, little actual progress on the assigned work is seen while the other things are being worked out.

The leader in the Forming stage needs to orient the team to the task at hand. For this stage of the process, the leader needs to show up as a skilled organizer. There needs to be a clear explanation of the task and a good discussion process that brings out any concerns or questions. It is imperative that the leader not believe that silence equates with agreement or understanding. Going around the room or reaching out to team members individually later to confirm that understanding has been achieved can save a lot of grief later. The leader also needs to be aware of the emotional dynamics that are beginning. While some conflict in these early stages is inevitable as these relationships find equilibrium, the leader can influence how hard or easy that conflict will be to manage. The leader needs to be sensitive to the engagement process that is happening. They can look for and emphasize those characteristics that will support the formation of in-group connections in the team. They must take the lead role in setting clear expectations. They need to be careful with status considerations. In order to engage the team, all team members need to have positive feelings about their status in the team. On the other hand, anything that creates a status gap between team members may exaggerate conflict in the next stage of team development. An example might be publicly making a bit too much of someone joining the team, someone the leader hoped would join but was unsure they would. Celebrating individual achievements and successes can be a binding force in later stages of team development but making people "special" before any work is done can sow division.

Assigning roles within the task is an important part of the leader role of the Forming team. It is also one of the most common sources of confusion and discord. The leader leaves the first meeting believing their instructions were clear. At the second meeting, they find little accomplished and total confusion as to who was doing what. The driver of this all-too-common situation is the discrepancy between where the focus of the leader and that of the team were during that meeting. The leader often comes focused on the task. The team often comes focused on the team engagement and dynamics, even if unconsciously. As I have discussed in previous chapters, the neural systems behind engagement are powerful. They can be quite disruptive of more intellectual processes.

One way to counter this is to put some extra effort into task clarity, including creating a clear visual record of sub task assignment. A useful tool for this is the RACI tool, standing for Responsible, Accountable, Consulted, and Informed. This tool is widely used in business, but in my experience, has had only patchy uptake in healthcare. These are the four elements, in order of a usual hierarchy:

- **Accountable** - This person is the one held to account by a higher authority that the work is done, even if they are not the person with their hands on the task. In many teams, this letter will be most frequently assigned to the leader.

- **Responsible** - This is the designation for those who do the specific work. Sometimes, this may be the same as the person who is accountable.

- **Consulted** - This describes those who may not be involved in the entirety of the task but are required to offer some support at some point in the process. Some writers refer to this category as "Contributors"

- **Informed** - These individuals are not involved in a specific sub task but need some awareness of it to work within the team or coordinate with other tasks.

The power of this approach lies not so much in the clarity of the categories but in the fact that it creates information that is very easy to record and display in simple tables (Table 3).

Table 3.

	Johann	Mary	Sushila	David	Ken
Sub Task 1	I	R	R	C	A
Sub Task 2	I	C	I	I	A, R
Sub Task 3	R	C	C	C	A
Sub Task 4	C	I	C	R	A

Example of a RACI Table

The information can also be included in meeting minutes and agendas by listing the name behind each item, followed by the appropriate RACI initial. Not only does this create a clear visual record of the sub-task assignments but the leader can also use this in meeting preparation. As I discussed in the chapter on meetings, setting aside some time before a meeting to send gentle reminders of important contributions that will be required is time well spent.

If the members of the team aren't well known to the leader, it's important at this stage to get some measure of the skills that individual team members bring to the project. Leaving some time in an initial meeting for team members to introduce themselves and their interests is wise.

Having assigned roles and tasks, the leader's work is not yet complete. Now is the time to use, or at least offer, the process for task delegation that I outlined in an earlier chapter. Set up some time to check with individuals or subgroups after the initial team meeting to confirm clarity on the task, deal with questions that arise, confirm a timetable for reporting back, define individual autonomy, and determine the type of feedback the person or group would find most useful. This investment of time at the front end can save huge amounts of time and effort further into the process.

Leading a Storming Team: Building Trust

After a short initial period where things seem calm and in order, teams enter the Storming phase. Team members may begin to question the purpose, the methods chosen, and even the competence of the leader. They test the boundaries around their assigned roles. There may be open conflict. Factions may form or declare themselves and jockey for position to show that they're more important and worthy of attention than others. Leaders may notice less overt but equally negative behaviours, such as triangulation, where team members gossip and scheme between each other about other team members, without ever bringing their concerns out in a face-to-face meeting. The inter-personal dynamics begin to consume the team's bandwidth and energy. Productivity declines or halts as all the team's energy is focused on relationships rather than task. Sadly, many teams get stuck here. They either fester for months or years, achieving little, or break up as a failed experiment.

Anyone who's had the experience of parenting toddlers or teenagers may recognize the pattern above. Just like parenting in those situations, trying to manage by just repeating what you did in the Forming phase, only louder, will not work. A parent in those situations needs to give the emerging voice and identity in the child room to emerge while maintaining reasonable boundaries. The leader of a Storming team has a similar role. They need to keep the team's purpose and goals visible and use their conversation and conflict skills to ensure that everyone is being heard and that conflict is being surfaced. The leader now moves from a directorial role to one that's more coach-like. In Forming, the leader tends to lead by providing clear and detailed direction; in Storming, the leader tends to lead with questions and inquiry. These coaching activities focus on relationship building within the team.

This is the stage where dysfunctional team behaviours can take root. A useful schema of dysfunctional team behaviours is that described by Patrick Lencioni in his book *The 5 Dysfunctions of a Team*. The book is written as narrative fable about a fictitious company. In addition to underscoring the dysfunctions in the title, it's interesting to follow the actions of the fictitious CEO and map them on to the engagement strate-gies mentioned earlier in the book. Lencioni expresses his dysfunctions as a pyramid, with the dysfunctions forming layers, and each layer being associated with a behaviour that is visible in the team members. At the base of the pyramid, underpinning everything else, is lack of trust. This is associated with team members presenting themselves as invulner-able and not acknowledging their weaknesses. It's a concept strongly supported by Brené Brown's research, which emphasized the necessity of expressing vulnerability in the building of trust. The next layer is fear of conflict. This can manifest as artificial harmony. Conflict isn't seen in team meetings, but once outside the door, the gossip, triangulation, and sometimes, frank sabotage begin. Building on that is lack of commit-ment. Team members remain ambiguous around decisions and resist finding any agreement that will commit them to a course of action. Next is avoidance of accountability. The team will pull its standards down to whatever is happening rather than strive to achieve something that might be out of reach and risks failure. The top of the pyramid is inat-tention to results. This is manifest as team members acting to enhance their own status and massaging their own egos at the expense of the team's performance.

Many of the approaches already sampled in this book can help a leader with the conversations around the upper layers of the pyramid. More nuanced approaches can be found in the "further reading" section. Dealing with the base of the structure, however, building trust in a team warrants some extra attention.

One of the most widely referenced programs on developing trust in the workplace, including healthcare workplaces, is Stephen M.R. Covey's *The Speed of Trust*. Covey's successful book and training program conceive that trust is anchored in self trust, which then extends into relation-ship trust and onward into organizational, market, and societal trust. The model is quite complex, and in addition to the book, is supported by worksheets, workbooks, and a thick deck of concept cards. Covey posits that self trust is based in credibility, which is built on four cores: Integrity, Intent, Capabilities, and Results. Each of these cores have subcomponents that align well with the attributes quoted in earlier chapters to support leader credibility with followers.

Relationship trust relies on thirteen trust-building behaviours, many of which align with concepts mentioned in previous chapters in the context of followership and significant conversations. Groups trained in this method are encouraged to reflect on one or more of the cores of behaviours at each of their meetings. This system is useful for teams with a stable composition who engage on a regular basis, but it can be more challenging to apply to more ad hoc arrangements. That said, physician leaders may find the framework personally helpful in informing their own trust-building behaviour, even if they choose not to attempt to implement the system across the team.

Brené Brown suggests a simpler framework of agreed behaviours within a team to promote trust building: the BRAVING model. The acronym stands for Boundaries, Reliability, Accountability, Vault, Integrity, Nonjudgement, and Generosity. Boundaries refers to respecting each other's personal boundaries and being willing to ask when unsure about a boundary. Reliability is about living up to one's commitments. Accountability requires owning, apologizing, and making amends where possible for one's errors. Vault means only sharing information that is yours to share. Integrity refers to doing what's right rather than what's easy or convenient. Nonjudgement means that team members can describe their experiences and wants without judgement. Generosity suggests that, where there is ambiguity, the most generous interpretation of events will be considered first. She provides a convenient one-page document on her website that can be used as part of a team's terms of reference or working rules. My one caution is that the document is largely written in the second person, with many more "you" statements than "I" or "we" statements. This might not be quite the right tone for environments that are already sensitized to conflict. Paraphrasing the concepts into "we" statements may be helpful before presenting it to a team.

Leading a Norming Team: Building Confidence

The Norming team is finding a way past its conflicts and uncertainties. Team members are responding to the leader's coaching and becoming more focused on appreciating each other's abilities than criticizing their perceived deficiencies. Team members see positive value in being part of the team. The team now starts to become more productive and confident. Differences of opinion are aired openly and resolved. The team begins to focus and debate ways of getting things done, rather than just challenging the wisdom of doing them. The leader now needs to step back from directive behaviour and look for opportunities to gradually surrender autonomy to the team. Micromanaging the team, which may have been appropriate in the Forming phase, in this phase will generate frustration and resentment. Team members should be encouraged to be creative and problem solve. The leader needs to accept that growth of the team may require some tolerance for failure. The coach-like behaviours of the Storming phase remain appropriate, but now the coaching is about helping team members fulfil their potential rather than navigating relationships. The leader collaborates with the team and is willing to accept their decisions on some matters. The team begins to do more relationship building beyond the team rather than just within it.

Leading a Performing Team: Building Excellence

The team is now achieving its goals. Individual team members understand and respect each other's roles. They adapt to day-to-day challenges and problem solve effectively. The leader isn't needed to direct normal activities and is free to look at the team's potential through more of a strategic lens. The leader at this stage plays the role of champion, ensuring the team gets the recognition it deserves and continues to have the resources it needs. But the leader should also be a visionary, looking for new challenges that will align with what the team has become, and keep them stimulated and fresh.

This is now the time the leader may want to begin thinking about succession-planning for team leadership. One of the challenges that's very draining for physician leaders is that they're frequently called upon to form and lead multiple teams and committees. There comes a point when this is unsustainable unless part of the development plan is to train or develop someone to take on the team once the work has begun. While some teams are clearly part of a leader's mandate, ad hoc teams, working groups, and the like need not become an albatross around the leader's neck. Physician leaders should, wherever possible, use these as opportunities to bring on other leaders. Trying to rotate chairing meetings or delegating the meeting to someone else when the leader has other pressing matters are good ways of exploring the leadership ability of team members.

Leading an Evolving Team: Adapting to Change

At the time that Tuckman added the Adjourning stage, the concept being captured was that of a team ending and breaking up upon completion of its mandate. The contemporary reality is more complex. It's now normal for the tenure of people in roles that bring them to teams to be shorter than the life of the team. We're living in a time of unprecedented mobility within and between organizations, even for physicians. As such, teams now tend to experience many "endings" as the members turn over and move on to other roles.

The ending of teams has been associated with the stages of grieving. When a person with whom a team has formed connections leaves, the leader must make space for the emotions that will follow for at least some team members and allow some conversation room for it. Failing to do so may result in anger, a common initial reaction to loss. If this hasn't been allowed to surface, even if that means it's directed at the leader, there's a risk it will be the first thing received by new team members. It's not easy to come back from that sort of start in a new team. Leaders may need to be ready to manage some anger themselves if the departure threatens the stability or productivity of the team the leader has worked so hard to build. It's also important to keep in mind that mobility can work in two directions; it also increases the probability that an experienced team member may also be willing to return at some point in the future. Whatever your initial emotional reaction, accepting someone's decision to leave with some degree of Zen and wishing them well in their future efforts is always a safe course.

Physician leaders do need to watch for patterns in departures from teams, however. Talented people moving on to clearly bigger challenges, better pay, or other positive alignments are one thing. People taking the first exit door when there really doesn't seem to be a personal advantage is something else. It's a sign of trouble and needs investigation. Leaders need to recognize that they can be the problem. As mentioned earlier in this article, physician leaders are given few opportunities for in-depth learning and practice in working with teams. It's not unusual for them to stumble on the way and need expert and experienced help.

The level of turnover that is now the norm in most organizations means that physician leaders can assume they will often be leading teams in which members are at different points in the team-development journey. The leader now requires something of a chameleon-like presence, which needs some intellectual gymnastics. They need to be the organizer and then coach to the new person, coach and confidant to the grieving, while still being champion and visionary to the whole team. Some dedicated time commitment to the new team member is required. But when integrating someone into the high-performing team, the leader no longer must do it alone. They now can use a "buddy" system with existing and experienced team members. This supports the development of social connections required for engagement and is an opportunity to develop leadership skills in the more experienced team member. Where a reasonable degree of turnover is predictable, the leader can have the team put some collective effort into an onboarding process with standard sets of documentation, meetings with individuals or subgroups, or briefings about critical processes. This type of effort is both supportive of new members and a good way of creating some autonomy and control for the team over this type of change.

A more detailed approach to team development that factors in both the stage of the team and state of preparedness of individual members can be found in the Harvard Situational Leadership model. A practical summary of this can be found in the relevant volume of their One Minute Manager series that is listed in the "Further Reading" section.

A little later, Susan and Rosalind are still poring over the laptop ...

"Okay, I get it," Rosalind says. "Pretty much all teams are going to go through a phase where everyone is figuring out who they can trust and what they're doing there. So, what am I supposed to do about getting the work done while they figure it out?"

"I would say getting them to work together may be part of the work. What do you think you should do about it?" Susan replies.

Rosalind thinks for a minute. "Well, I guess just repeating history and holding the same meeting over and over again isn't going to get us any-where. That's like the old saying that insanity is doing the same thing over again and expecting to get a different result. I should start with the two folks who are being really cranky."

"And what will you do with them?"

Rosalind remains thoughtful. "I think I need to talk to them one-on-one and let them know how their behaviour is landing on me. Then I'll ask what it will take to get them to look positively at this, or even if they can. My physician-conduct conversation a couple of weeks ago went better than I thought, so I do feel a bit more confident after Jim's coaching in being more direct with this stuff."

"Anything else?"

"I suppose it's not a bad idea to have a quick chat with everyone on the committee, for that matter, to see what they need to move forward on this. I don't want to be seen to be just attending to squeaky wheels. Once I have some idea of what's getting under people's skin, maybe we need to spend some meeting time on that. Maybe we should put rewriting terms of refer-ence and policies on the backburner until the group is aligned a bit better."

"Is there anywhere you can get help on this, or are you going to do the usual Wonder Woman act?"

Rosalind pulls a face at her. "I'll have you know I was just remembering that the regional Organizational Development group does stuff on managing teams. I was just about to say I would call them and see if they have any advice!"

"Yeah, right. But it does sound like a better approach than trying to break our doors. Now let's see if we can't find some good books for you on this."

Key Learnings

- *Think of teams as lifeforms with their own developmental trajectory.*

- *Recognize that teams need time to understand their purpose, establish status, develop trust and interdependency, and then move on to accomplish their tasks.*

- *Be ready to change your leadership approach as the team develops:*

    - *direct and provide role clarity to the newly formed team;*

    - *coach relationships using conversation and conflict skills for the team resolving trust and status;*

    - *coach task and skills using motivation and delegation skills for the team learning to align and perform;*

    - *champion and celebrate the mature, effective team;*

    - *manage the anxiety and grief of an ending or changing team.*

- *Have an intentional strategy for trust building in your team.*

- *Prepare to be nimble when team members move in and out and are at different stages of development in their team roles.*

FURTHER READING

Bruce W. Tuckman, "Developmental Sequence in Small Groups," *Psychological Bulletin,* 63(1965): 384–399.

Bruce W. Tuckman and Mary Ann Jensen, "Stages of Small Group Development Revisited," *Group Organizational Studies,* 2 (1977): 419–427.

Mindtools Content Team. "Forming, Storming, Norming and Performing. Tuckman's Model for Nurturing a Team to High Performance," July 15, 2021, https://www.mindtools.com/pages/article/newLDR_86.htm.

Tom Costello, "RACI-Getting Projects 'Unstuck,'" *ITPro* March/April (2012): 62–64.

Stephen M.R. Covey and Rebecca R. Merrill, *The Speed of Trust. The One Thing That Changes Everything (*New York, NY: Free Press, 2006).

Brené Brown, "The BRAVING Inventory," July 15, 2021, https://daretolead.brenebrown.com/workbook-art-pics-glossary/.

Ken Blanchard, Donald Carew, and Eunice Parisi-Carew, *The One Minute Manager Builds High Performing Teams* (New York, NY: William Morrow, 2009).

I DON'T HAVE TIME FOR THIS!

Sanjay comes home just after 7:00 p.m. He finds his twelve-year-old daughter, Sushila, sitting at the kitchen table, playing video games on her mother's laptop. "Mom said your dinner is in the microwave," she says by way of welcome, without looking up.

"Hi, Sue. Where is Mom?"

Sushila looks up and gives him a practised eye-roll. "Parent-teacher interviews for David. I think she sort of, like, expected you to be home in time to go to them."

Sanjay groans inwardly. He had said he would go, but that conversation was three days ago. He'd been out early and home late every day since, and it hadn't come up again. Evelyn would not be happy when she got home.

Evelyn comes in about an hour later. Sanjay starts to apologize but she cuts him off. "We'll talk about it later, when the kids are in bed."

About nine o'clock, Evelyn pokes her head into the den where he's working on the computer and says, "Join me for a cup of tea?"

They sit down in the kitchen. Sanjay is expecting the worst. Evelyn looks up and sighs. "David was pretty disappointed tonight. I think you're going to have to find some way to make it up to him. Some of the group-project work he did was on display. It was really pretty good."

Sanjay is now feeling pretty defensive. "I know. I'm sorry. But there's just a lot of important stuff happening, and clinic has been really busy."

Evelyn smiles. "I know, and I do appreciate that what you do is important. I really do. I don't want to have a fight about that. But it's not the only thing that's important. You remember when you were thinking about taking this job? I did ask how you would make it work, given that you were already so busy. I don't think I got a clear answer. Well, look at this week. You were on call last weekend; we hardly saw you then. You missed both kids' soccer games. You've missed dinner and breakfast with us three days in a row. Is this what it will be like from here on in?"

It's now Sanjay's turn to sigh. "I guess I didn't expect it to be quite this crazy. Other department heads are doing similar work, and I don't want to be the one to be seen complaining."

"Ah, the great macho doctor thing again. Selfless, tireless martyrs saving the world!"

"I don't think being sarcastic is going to help," Sanjay replies, more than a little stung.

"But don't you see that's how it looks? And are you sure those other department heads haven't found other ways to make it work? Have you asked them?"

"Well ... no," Sanjay sheepishly admits.

Evelyn gets up and fetches a pad of paper and a pen. "Okay, I'm taking off the wife hat now and putting on my counselling hat. And we're going to talk about this right now for as long as it takes."

Better time management is an almost universal wish of physician leaders. Taking control of our time is essential for our own effectiveness and well being. Also, one of the most common challenges of recruiting people to those leadership positions is "I'm not sure if I can find the time." To attract other physicians to leadership, physician leaders must demonstrate by example that the demands of leadership can be managed within a reasonable lifestyle.

Mastery of time occurs in four steps. The first is understanding our own individual perception of time. The second is understanding that our energy and abilities vary in time. Next is the allocation of our time based upon insight into what is truly urgent and important. Finally, physician leaders must be able to hold themselves accountable to applying those insights to their decision making around the use of their valuable time.

The Experience of Time

Thinking about time can quickly become a bit mind bending. There are occasions when clocks seem to be full of glue and minutes, hours and days drag by. At the other extreme, sometimes we become so engaged in an activity or train of thought that we become completely unaware of the passage of time. This state, the subject of writing and research by the psychologist Mihaly Csikszentmihalyi, has been called "flow." Our experience of the rate of time is highly subjective and variable. Where on the time continuum—past, present, or future—our consciousness tends to focus can be quite varied and is unique for all of us. Dr. Philip Zimbardo, over decades of research into how we perceive time, has identified five "temporal frames" that capture how we cluster our time perceptions:

- **Past-Negative** - In this frame, the past is a place of unhappy experiences that imbue us with pessimism. It's a place we go to ruminate on what has been wrong in our lives.

- **Past-Positive** - This is the past place of nostalgia. The past is better than the present and remembered with fondness and perhaps wistfulness.

- **Present-Fatalistic** - This aligns with a metaphor of time as a fast-flowing river that sweeps us along through events that we cannot control. We must suffer whatever comes our way.

- **Present Hedonistic** - Here we eat, drink, and be merry and do not consider what is coming around the corner.

- **Future** - Here we plan and consider diverging possibilities.

This is not abstract philosophy; the tendency to dwell in each of these frames can be measured by a validated online inventory tool. The link can be found in the "Further Reading" section. Based on accumulating data from this inventory and studies correlating the inventory with other psychological measures, the researchers have proposed an ideal balance between these frames not just for time issues but for contributing to having a well-balanced emotional state.

How our brains structure the way we experience time is an important influence on both our emotions and our productivity. Predominant focus in past negative, present fatalistic, and future have been associated with risk of depression and anxiety, whereas past positive and present hedonistic are correlated with positive emotions. To be productive in the present and organized for the future, we must accept what is beyond our control in the present, while making room in the moment for our happiness, well being, and celebration of achievement. We also need some forward-thinking plans. We must avoid, however, obsessing about the future. Such a focus can result in being paralysed, unable to decide between an infinity of possible future outcomes. If our minds lean excessively to past or future, we risk not allocating enough time to present events. Conversely, if we fill every minute of our schedule with concerns imposed by work, we leave no room for when we inevitably drift for some time into reminiscence or speculation. We also risk losing perspective on our minute-to-minute experience and becoming overwhelmed. At that point, we are living in the Present-Fatalistic, letting external circumstance control us.

In balanced time perception, making allowance for appropriate time spent in past, present, and future is essential. Some allocation of our mental space to Present-Hedonistic, to just sit back and smell the roses, is essential. Achieving this balance in perception is amenable to a range of coaching or self-change approaches discussion, which is beyond the scope here. The article in the "Further Reading" section by the British psychologist and coach Dr. Ilona Boniwell is a good resource for those interested in exploring this further. Without such balance, we may pay lip service to managing time in a logical way, but our preferred time focus will act to sabotage our best efforts. The importance of physician leaders being self-aware has been raised often; this is another dimension of it.

When Is the Best Time?

Physician leaders should be familiar from their clinical work with the concept of diurnal variation. Unless you're an underground dwelling creature, the cycle of sun rising and setting is stamped on your biology. Comments about someone being a night person or a morning person are frequently made. This is a real phenomenon with implications for physician leadership. We have a complex array of circadian rhythms that are controlled in part by neurons in the suprachiasmatic nucleus of the hypothalamus, but also by molecular mechanisms that are widely distributed through different tissue types. These rhythms change during our life cycles, as anyone whose lived experience includes getting a teenager out of bed in time for school can attest. We often think of the schedules we adopt as habits, but the biology behind them is largely innate and not easily changed. Research has shown the brain stubbornly sticking to a twenty-four-hour cycle when people are forced into different day lengths, such as occurs with physicians on busy call schedules. Circumstances may force us to find ways to work against our natural rhythms; this can have cognitive, emotional, and possibly health consequences.

Much of our understanding of the chronobiology comes from the work of Till Roenneberg and Martha Merrow. Using a tool they developed, the Munich Chronotype Questionnaire, they've been able to map different chronotypes onto the day. Their results certainly confirm the existence of "larks," who appear to be at their best very early in the day, and "owls," who are at their best late. The former is about 14 percent and the latter 21 percent of the populations, so most of us fall somewhere in between. This classification is largely based on the midpoint of sleep. Our physiology and behaviour are more closely linked to the number of hours since waking than the time of day. The larks and "third birds," as the author Daniel Pink has characterized the in-between group who together make up almost 80 per cent of the population, have that midpoint tightly clustered within midnight to 6:00 a.m. This means our population is skewed toward people who tend to be at their peak early in the day rather than late. Research has shown that this influences several important areas, of which physician leaders should be aware:

- **Mood follows a daily pattern** - For most people, mood peaks in the morning, declines in the afternoon, and rises again in the evening. This may be displaced later for the roughly one in five people who are true owls.

- **Ability to perform analytical and precision tasks follows a daily pattern** - Tasks that require logical processes or following procedures tend to be more successfully accomplished in a similar pattern with mood, with better performance earlier in the day and later, with an afternoon dip in between. This period was termed the "optimal" time of day by early researchers. Again, "owls" will tend to follow a reverse pattern. Some studies have suggested that the precision and accuracy of medical procedures, like colonoscopies, are influenced by this pattern, but the literature contains a lot of conflicting results. Much of the application of this idea to medicine has been based on retrospective studies, and methodological issues do cast some doubt on some of the conclusions. Research that is both prospective and based on measured chronotypes of physicians rather than time of day does not yet seem to exist.

- **Ability to perform creative and inferential tasks follows a different daily pattern** - Marieke Wieth and Rose Zacks published a large study in 2011 in which they compared the ability of people grouped according to chronotype to solve problems that require insight. These are problems that are solved suddenly when the brain jumps to a non-obvious concept, versus analytical tasks where a logical process is followed to its conclusion. They found that for tasks that required imagination and inference, people tended to do better in the non-optimal time, reversing the pattern for analytical-type tasks. They hypothesized that, during these troughs, the inhibitory processes in the brain that help us resist distraction earlier in daily cycles are less active. While this compromises our ability to stay on logical tasks, it may help us with more creative ones.

- **People are less likely to make judgements based on stereotypes in the optimal time of day** - Galen Bodenhausen published research in 1990 that showed that when people were asked to review fictitious cases of student misconduct in association with certain stereotypes that suggested guilt, they were more likely to be swayed by the evidence during their optimal period of the day and more likely to follow the stereotype in their non-optimal period. He hypothesized that they were better able to resist the easy distraction of the stereotypes and focus on the evidence in their optimal time period. The physician leader can apply these concepts both to themselves and to the people on whom they must depend. If your optimal period is early in the day, that's when the tasks that require attention to detail should be performed. Situations in which a decision is important and needs to be based on more than emotion also belong there. But situations that need out-of-the-box thinking, such as brainstorming new programs or dealing with a conundrum that defies any sort of straight line "from here to there" may be better done in those trough times, which for larks and third birds would be early afternoon. Given the risks of poorer analysis at those times, it would be wise to use such sessions to generate options and then sleep on them and make decisions on another day in your optimal time.

In dealing with others, the physician leader needs to be aware of the impact of timing on both teams and individuals. It's easier when dealing with one person to recognize their diurnal pattern and time your interactions based on what you need from them. It's a bit harder in groups and teams; the odds are good that you'll have about 20 percent owls in any group; they will be perpetually out of synch with the others. One way out of this is to bounce things between the chronotype groups. Create situations in which the owls can look at the data on their time (evening and night) and others can do the analytical stuff in the morning. This is one thing that's being made easier by the virtual work environment and the proliferation of work patterns. When looking for brainstorming and creativity, make some space to bounce ideas around for a day or three so that people can do that work at a time when their head is in the right place. If you want everyone bright eyed and bushy tailed, avoid after lunch meetings. Leave people to work quietly on their own at those times!

Deciding Urgency and Importance

Urgency is an important influence in time-related decisions. Jon Elster, a political and social theorist, identifies that we tend to be "intolerant of inaction." He draws a distinction between two states that form that intolerance: impatience and urgency. In impatience, we are unable to defer gratification and will accept smaller gains for immediate reward. Urgency is more complicated; it leaves space for recalculation of the benefits of delay, and the urge to act may be tempered by other concerns. In both cases, our judgement is likely being influenced by how acting rewards us or reduces our anxiety. How many of the things that hit your urgent list will have serious consequences for you and others if delayed (meaning they are truly urgent)? Alternatively, how many things on that list will have irritating consequences or require some effort to defer or refuse, but whose delay will not contribute to the end of life as we know it? Here the reinforcement is often no more than avoiding or deferring something undesirable or requiring of more immediate effort to secure a longer-term gain. Such immediate gratifications can, unfortunately, still be powerful rewards.

Do you ever accept a task that's really a distraction, but it's easier to get it out of the way than deal with a nagging requester or have a significant conversation about whether the request was appropriate? Do you find yourself saying, "It's just easier to do it myself"? If you answered "yes" to either question, you may be confusing impatience with urgency. Physician leaders are busy people; as a result, many of their urgency rankings risk being relegated to Daniel Kahneman's largely subconscious System 1 thinking, which supports quick decisions based on unconsciously recognizing patterns of inputs. This instant decision making, while less effort in the moment, creates the risk of being seduced into short-term expediency at long-term cost. We take things on that we shouldn't because that's the easiest thing to do in the moment. Mastering time requires using Kahneman's more objective, intentional, and reflective System 2 thinking to make conscious decisions about what issues truly merit the designation "urgent."

The issue of importance also has layers of nuance. To quote Stephen R. Covey, "If something is important, it contributes to your mission, your values and your high priority goals."[3] The reflection on these that

---

3 Stephen R. Covey, *The 7 Habits of Highly Effective People. Powerful Lessons in Personal Change* (New York: Simon and Schuster, 1990): 151.

you were invited to do in the first chapter of this book was not just an academic exercise. How you allocate your precious time should be intimately connected to values, purpose or mission, and goals.

It's worth noting what research says about how we perceive time well spent. Dr. Ilona Boniwell found that time well spent was associated with doing things we liked, that served balance in our lives, worked well with our organizational systems, and didn't leave us with a sense of time running away from us and being out of our control. She describes this as a cycle that might be seen to reward some choices and discourage others. It does hinge on the starting point of doing things we like, or things that give us satisfaction. What gives us satisfaction can add another layer of complexity.

Dr. Kennon Sheldon found that events contributing to self esteem, autonomy, relatedness, and competence tended to be seen as the most satisfying and were consistently ahead of events contributing to self actualization, meaning, physical thriving, and popularity. His findings suggest that we unconsciously place our need for achievement ahead of our other needs. Events associated with acquisition of money and luxury were seen as an even less satisfying use of time. There's a little red flag here. Putting status and achievement ahead of wellbeing may well be relevant to the discussion of burnout among physicians and other high-achieving professionals. Finding enhanced self esteem more satisfying than self actualization and wellness suggests a possibly hardwired risk of making time choices to look good rather than pursuing personal goals. Physician leaders should regularly reflect on how they are allocating time and ask, "Why am I doing that?" Once again, the importance of self-awareness surfaces.

Being Accountable about Time

The core issue in mastering time is having a clear decision-making paradigm about allocating time and a clear action pathway arising from that paradigm. A very simple and effective model, described in detail under the third of Stephen Covey's *7 Habits of Highly Effective People* (Put First Things First), is the Eisenhower Box. This model was first described in a speech by President Eisenhower to the World Council of Churches in 1954. The box is a simple two-by-two grid with columns titled "Urgent" and "Not Urgent" and rows titled "Important" and "Not Important" (Figure 8). The simplest application suggests that tasks in the *urgent important* Quadrant 1 be done immediately. These are tasks that clearly fit your criteria for needing to be done and to be done now.

The Eisenhower Box	Urgent	Not Urgent
Important	Quadrant 1. Do Now!	Quadrant 2. Schedule
Not Important	Quadrant 3. Delegate, Defer, or Discard	Quadrant 4. Discard

Figure 8. The Eisenhower Box Approach to Time Management.

Tasks in the *not urgent, important* Quadrant 2, while important, can be scheduled to a convenient time. Tasks in the *urgent, not important* Quadrant 3 may be urgent for someone else other than you, or even if urgent, the penalty for not putting them ahead of other priorities may be acceptable. These may be deferred, delegated, or discarded. Tasks in the *not urgent, not important* Quadrant 4 may be nice to do but not essential, or often are tasks kept out of tradition or habit. These may be safely discarded.

Covey makes some further telling observations about the "highly effective" people he studied. The first is that they anticipate the demands of the *urgent, important* Quadrant 1. They pre-emptively allocate time for these tasks, knowing they will happen, even if they don't know what they will be. This is analogous to an office medical practice reserving a couple of appointments each day for urgent patients. Try blocking off several hours per week in your calendar for things that come up. Set it up so that only you can book into those times. You'll be surprised how quickly people around you get used to the idea that there are some blocks of time you're only available for genuine emergencies. Covey's second and most striking finding was that effective people simply do not do either Quadrant 3 or Quadrant 4 tasks. In his view, highly effective people focused exclusively on that which was important. It follows that they must be skilled at turning down requests for their time. Consider developing a script of "no" lines, such as:

- *"I'll need to think about that and get back to you."*

- *"I can't fit that in at the moment."*

- *"I need to look at this in more detail alongside other priorities before I can commit."*

- *"I think this would be better fit for___"*

- *"Rather than me just take this over, let's talk about what you would need to run with this."*

It may not seem comfortable saying "no" to your followers, but as a leader, you need to balance your duty to be effective with your desire to keep everyone happy. There must be compromise. If you take on too much and fail at everything, your relationship with followers will likely suffer much more than what will result from occasional polite rebuffs.

Totally ignoring the tasks allocated to Quadrant 3 may be a luxury not all can afford, but this area is a prime one for developing delegation skills. There is a trade off here; in exchange for gaining back the time spent on the task, the leader must intentionally allocate a share of Quadrant 2 time to provide clarity on the task to the delegate, make commitment to follow up, provide thoughtful and constructive feedback, and celebrate success. By so doing, you convert a distracting task to a capacity building exercise for members of your team that will reduce your workload in the long term. Delegation is also a valuable tool in deriving the most benefit from personal time. Several studies have shown that people who use their wealth to buy time for desired pursuits are happier than those who merely accumulate stuff, even if it's fancy and expensive stuff. This is the exception to the old maxim of money not buying happiness. Time spent in maintaining social relationships, fitness, and health should clearly be Quadrant 2 activities. If you're deferring these in your precious off time to cut grass or clean bathrooms, however, you might want to explore putting these mundane tasks in Quadrant 4 and buying those services.

At this point, I need to raise the most common time-management mistake that physician leaders make. They underestimate, or (surprisingly often) make no allowance whatsoever for the time that leadership needs. On many occasions, I've seen physicians sign leadership contracts requiring 0.5, 0.6, or even 0.8 of a full-time equivalent and make little or no adjustment to their existing, usually already more than full-time, clinical and/or academic schedules. This has only two outcomes: exhaustion if they honour the time commitment, and poor leadership if they fail to put in the necessary leadership time. This goes back to the concepts of why one should become a leader as discussed in the first chapter. Somewhere, consciously, sub-consciously, or unconsciously, you made a decision that taking a leadership role was an important way of achieving your goals and meeting your self-determination needs. That has consequences that include new things being added to the first and second quadrants of your Eisenhower box. This is only sustainable if you move things already in those quadrants into the Quadrant 3 and Quadrant 4. You need to be prepared to give things up. You need to be prepared for conversations with clinical colleagues about redistributing clinical and teaching loads; those may be challenging conversations. You need to be aware of and ready to protect what's important outside of work. Too often, this is what ends up giving in this situation. This is another very specific situation where working with a coach or mentor can be invaluable to help separate reality from your own self-image anxieties.

All of this is only going to work if physician leaders stick to their principles. This includes being self aware and consistent in making decisions about time allocation. It means being transparent in what does and does not work for you and saying no when it matters. Above all, it means using time to meet your goals and live to your purpose and values, while avoiding making choices based on anxiety about image or status.

Email: The New Thief of Time

Email gets a special mention because it's frequently identified as one of the major time stresses in many environments, including physicians and their leadership. It's recognized as a driver in many workplace distraction scenarios and maladaptive behaviours. Some companies and European countries have gone as far as regulation and legislation to limit out of hours access to and use of work email, as a workplace health and safety concern. Despite this imposition, these countries and companies seem to be doing fine, perhaps proving that there is life beyond email.

Physician leaders need to recognize that we get the behaviour we accept, and we get even more of the behaviour we reward. Do you sit at your screen at all hours, waiting to pounce upon and respond to messages at any time of the day and night? If so, you are training people to send you emails and expect a response instantaneously. If you touch "reply to all," you're inviting everyone to intrude on your time. You'll never get on top of email until you accept your own role in creating how much of a problem it is for you. You could, for example, set aside a specific time for email processing in your schedule and set up an automatic reply informing people of that. If you do so, you'll find that people will pick up the phone if it's really urgent (it usually isn't). They may just conclude that, if there won't be an instant response, maybe it's not important enough to waste time typing. It's possible to construct filters to align incoming messages with your urgent and important criteria, and it's important to not encourage long email dialogues. If you see one forming, send the message, "This would be better discussed in a meeting—let's set up a time." If an email doesn't need a response, don't send one just for the sake of it. Only send emails with useful information; it may seem a bit cold, but just thanking people for emailing you should not be automatic. Do those one or two hundred times per day and you've lost a lot of time.

Unfortunately, there's a darker side to the way in which email steals time: its capacity to create havoc. Emails are often written when we're alone with our thoughts. Before we had screens and keyboards, these times alone were when we could think the most outrageous things without penalty. By the time we returned to polite society, these thoughts had usually slunk back into the dark recesses of our minds, and we could converse using appropriate filters. Email gives them a path to escape, literally slipping through our fingers, before better judgement can intervene. From long experience, I have discovered five invariable and annoying properties of email as a form of communication.

1. If an email can be misconstrued in any way, however unlikely, it will be.

2. If a typo can catastrophically change the meaning of email, it will occur.

3. If an email will cause serious problems if read by a certain person or people, it will find its way to them.

4. No email can be deleted in a way that means it can never be found again.

5. There is no such thing as the last word with email.

It's now distressingly common for physician leaders to deal with conflict and disciplinary issues based on the unfiltered nature of email. Email lacks any of the non-verbal elements of communication that make most of the meaning developed in interactions between people. The content must be inhumanly precise to avoid the sense-making that sometimes creates wild stories in the minds of the readers. It's a great medium for setting up meetings, transferring non-controversial information, and sending short acknowledgements. Once the material moves into emotional territory, it almost always makes things worse.

As a physician leader, you will get emails that will make you see red. The correct sequence to respond is easy. First, do not respond! Second, wait until you can think about the message without completely seeing red—twenty-four hours is not a bad rule. Third, send this message, and only this message: "We need to talk." And send it only to the original sender; do not get sucked into the "reply to all" trap. Fourth, apply the techniques in the chapter on significant conversations. This will resolve the issue in far less time than you would lose when emotional emails turn something smouldering into a conflagration.

Email survival, detox, and rehab (yes, it does meet the criteria for addictive behaviour for some) is a big topic and is well covered in the book *The Hamster Revolution*, included in the "Further Reading" section at the end of this article.

There is no instant panacea for time management. Each of these steps requires reflection, development of a process that works for you, commitment to apply that process, and re-evaluation of your results. It involves discarding old habits and developing new ones, with all the neuropsychological complexity that we now understand comes with such changes. Not surprisingly, this is one area of leadership in which working with a coach can be most helpful.

Meanwhile, it is now 11.30 p.m. at Sanjay's house, and he and Evelyn have made some decisions ...

Evelyn looks down at the now rather imposing list of notes she has made.

"Okay, Sanjay, this is what we've agreed on. You're going to look for someone to take over one day per week of your office clinic. You think one of the docs who's talking about slowing down might see that as a good way of easing out, at least for the next year or two. We'll take a financial hit for that, and I know we're hoping for a trip to India soon. But if we keep our current cars another year and be a bit careful on some other fronts, we can make it work.

"You're going to let me contact your assistant, Jan, directly to get her to put family commitments into your office and hospital calendars as "private" entries, blocking those times, so no one can slip something else in unless we

agree to it. You're going to talk to the group about allowing some schedule shuffling so that you don't end up with evening department-head meetings right after being on call.

"At home, we're going to start getting up together at 5.45 a.m. Monday to Thursday. I'll get up with you and make coffee. I'll do my yoga and exercises; this will be an incentive for me to do that regularly again! You'll have an uninterrupted hour at the computer to write, prepare for meetings, do medical-record stuff, whatever. We can hold each other accountable and get a bit more talk time. You can do an hour of work in the evening and two hours on weekend days at a time that doesn't conflict with something we're doing as a family, but other than call nights, you're ours the rest of the time when you're at home.

"You're going to look for some courses, books, whatever on time-management ideas to try to get more of your work done at work.

"We're going to try this out for three months. If things don't improve, you agree that you will not renew the department-head contract when it comes up for renewal. Does that sound right and fair?"

Sanjay is quite relieved and grateful. He's sure he couldn't have handled this as effectively as Evelyn. "That sounds really good, and thanks. Maybe we should swap jobs?"

Evelyn grins. "No thanks. I'm quite happy where I am. But just to strike while the iron is hot, your mother called today, reminding me that she and your dad are involved with the local planning for Karthika Deepam next month, and she wants your help. You better start by putting some time aside for that, or she'll have you seeing stars that aren't part of the festival!"

Sanjay grinned. "It'll be in the calendar before I go to work tomorrow!"

Key Learnings

- *Understand how you perceive time and how that affects the way you manage it.*

- *Have one master schedule that covers all aspects of your life.*

- *Be aware of your diurnal rhythms and of those with whom you must work closely; know the best times to perform certain tasks.*

- *Know what is important to you, both in and beyond work.*

- *Distinguish clearly that which is truly urgent.*

- *Allocate your time based on importance and urgency; leave some space for the unexpected.*

- *Have strategies for saying "No!"*

- *Be prepared to discard, delegate, or defer tasks that do not meet your importance or urgency criteria.*

- *Do not be a slave to email or other technological monsters.*

FURTHER READING

The Experience of Time

Philip G. Zimbardo, and John N. Boyd, "Putting Time in Perspective: A Valid, Reliable Individual-Differences Metric," *Journal of Personality and Social Psychology,* 77, Issue 6 (1999): 1271–1288.

Philip G. Zimbardo and John N. Boyd, "The Time Paradox. Zimbardo Time Perspective Inventory," July 1, 2021, http://www.thetimeparadox.com/zimbardo-time-perspective-inventory/.

Ilona Boniwell, Evgeny Osin, and Anna Sircova, "Introducing Time Perspective Coaching: A New Approach to Improve Time Management and Enhance

Well-being," *International Journal of Evidence Based Coaching and Mentoring,* 12, Issue 2 (2014): 24–40.

When Is the Best Time?

Daniel Pink, *When. The Scientific Secrets of Perfect Timing* (New York, NY: Riverhead Books, 2018).

Till Roenneberg, Anna Wirz-Justice, and Martha Merrow, "Life between Clocks: Daily Temporal Patterns of Human Chronotypes," *Journal of Biological Rhythms,* 18, Issue 1 (2003): 80–90.

Till Roenneberg and Martha Merrow, "Circadian Clocks—The Fall and Rise of Physiology," *Nature Reviews: Molecular Cell Biology,* 6 (2005): 965–971.

Marieke B. Wieth and Rose T. Zacks, "Time of Day Effects on Problem Solving: When the Non-optimal Is Optimal," *Thinking & Reasoning,* 17, Issue 4 (2011): 387–401.

Galen V. Bodenhausen, "Stereotypes as Judgmental Heuristics: Evidence of Circadian Variations in Discrimination," *Psychological Science,* 1(1990): 319–322.

Deciding Urgency and Importance

Jon Elster, "Urgency," *Inquiry,* 52(2009): 399–411.

Daniel Kahneman, *Thinking Fast and Slow* (Toronto, ON: Anchor Canada, 2011).

Kennon M. Sheldon, Andrew J. Elliot, Youngmee Kim, and Tim Kasser, "What Is Satisfying about Satisfying Events? Testing 10 Candidate Psychological Needs," *Journal of Personality and Social Psychology,* 80 (2001): 325–339.

Being Accountable about Time

Stephen R. Covey, *The 7 Habits of Highly Effective People* (New York, NY: Fireside, 1990).

Ashley V. Whillans, Elizabeth W. Dunn, Paul Smeets, Rene Bekkers, and Michael I. Morton, "Buying Time Promotes Happiness," *Proceedings National Academy of Sciences USA,* 114 (2017): 8523–8527.

Email: The New Thief of Time

Emma Russell, "Dealing with Work Email: What Are We Doing and Why Are We Doing It?" in *Making a Difference with Psychology*, eds. K. Niven, S. Lewis, and C. Kagan (Manchester: Richard Benjamin Trust, 2017): 202–209.

Mike Song, Vicki Halsey, and Tim Burress, *The Hamster Revolution. Stop Info-Glut—Reclaim Your Life* (San Francisco, CA: Berrett-Koehler Publishers, 2008).

IS IT JUST ME, OR IS THERE SOMETHING BURNING?

Rosalind comes into her office on Monday morning after a weekend off and is stopped by Anita, her assistant. "Hi, Rosalind. Andy from ER stuck his head in a few minutes ago, saying he needed to talk to you urgently. He looked a bit upset. He said to just call him on his cell phone."

Rosalind is a bit concerned. Andy took over from her as the ER Head, and his calm is legendary. She calls him as soon as she gets to her desk.

"Hi, Andy, what's up?"

"Hi, Rosalind, thanks for calling back so quickly. The short version is I need to know if you can pick up some shifts for the next few weeks while I look for a locum. The long version is we need to talk about Derek."

"I can certainly look at my schedule. I'm sure I can squeeze something in. But why do we need a locum now? And what's happening with Derek?"

Derek is a very experienced rural emergency physician, one of only two in town who are formally trained and certified as ER physicians rather than being a family doctor with an additional ER course certification. He's in his mid-fifties, has a son and daughter at university, and has been the department workhorse for years, always being the person doing the most shifts. He also does a lot of work as a course medical director for advanced life support training for rural physicians, which has him travelling a lot on his non-ER days. He is rather gruff but massively respected.

"He's gone."

"He's what?"

"He's gone. He sent me an email yesterday, with a letter from his GP attached, recommending he stop work immediately on health grounds. No

explanation what they were. He apologized for not being able to do his shifts for the next three weeks in the current schedule, and that was it. He's not answering his phone. So, I have ten shifts to fill now in the next three weeks, and I have to rejuggle next month's, which I was just about to send out."

"You don't think he's done ... something drastic?"

"This is pretty drastic, don't you think? But his wife is at home. I think we would have heard if there was anything ... serious."

Rosalind sighs. "Thanks, Andy. I have his number. I'll reach out. Send out a list of shifts we need filled, and I'll see what I can do. In the interim, let's just tell people Derek has had an emergency and leave it that for now."

She tries Derek's number a few times, but it just goes to voicemail. She leaves a couple of messages and then has a thought. She calls Susan.

"Hi, Susan. You did some work for an accountant, Bronwen, who's married to Derek, one of ER docs a little while ago, right?"

"Yes. In fact, she wants a few tweaks on her website. I just haven't gotten around to it yet."

"Any chance you could give her a call and just ... sort of check in?"

"That sounds a bit sinister. What's up?"

"I'm not sure I can say much, but people are bit concerned that things are okay with her husband."

"Okay, soul of discretion, that's me! I'll call you a little later."

About an hour later, Susan calls back.

"So much for subterfuge. Her first comment was she was expecting you to ask me to call her! They're preparing for a road trip, and everyone is safe and sound, but she said she will talk to Derek about giving you a call."

Few topics in modern healthcare have generated as much talk and as little action as burnout amongst healthcare professionals. It's a phenomenon that costs health systems dearly in people, safety, quality, and money. Burnout is a social process, not a mental illness, although mental illness can be one of its outcomes. The high rates seen amongst frontline healthcare professionals are an excellent example of "every system is perfectly designed to get the results it gets."

No one coaching healthcare professionals can do so without touching on burnout, or its opposite number, sustainable engagement in the work.

While the systems we work in, and to some extent the people we select to work in them, conspire to make this so common, every journey toward or away from burnout is a personal one. The purpose of this chapter is to introduce some of the terms and concepts in this territory. I'm not giving (indeed *cannot* give) you "The Answer." My hope is that this will provide you with a starting point for your own efforts to understand and manage this in your life and for those you lead.

Burnout: History and Meaning

The application of the term "burnout" appeared in 1970s America. It referred to a triad of emotional exhaustion, depersonalization or loss of compassion or connection with the people one serves, and a perception that one's efforts are increasingly ineffective and futile. The exact origin is hard to pinpoint, but the word seems to have crept into the literature from descriptions of social disintegration of chronic drug users, by being applied to those who were providing care for them. Literature dating back to the nineteenth century is replete with examples of characters demonstrating the beliefs and behaviours of burnout; it certainly existed before a term was invented for it. In 1981, Christina Maslach and Susan Jackson published an instrument for measuring "experienced burnout" by using questions to develop scores under three categories: emotional exhaustion, depersonalization, and personal accomplishment. It was called the Maslach Burnout Inventory (MBI). The amount of work in developing and validating this instrument was remarkable.

Certainly, having a tool to measure something is a good way to get people to measure it. Even now, forty years later, there are dozens of new publications each week within medicine alone referring to this instrument, or other derivatives of it, being used to score burnout in some small healthcare group or other. Sadly, papers using the inventory before and after testing an intervention to reduce burnout are orders of magnitude less common. It has become like the weather: a rich source of observation and conversation, but little effort is made to change it. Without getting into an endless debate about exact statistics, this growing crush of papers is not changing the basic story identified two or three decades ago. At any given moment, around 40 percent (and possibly more) of frontline healthcare workers show a significant score in at least one dimension of burnout. At some point in their careers, most of such workers will experience some degree of burnout measured in this way.

There are, however, compelling reasons to expect that burnout is increasing, even if one must be careful interpreting the research and statistics. On the societal side, the twentieth century and into the twenty-first has seen increasing individualization and weakening of ties into family and small social groups. We increasingly look to get our needs met from larger, more impersonal institutions. We're no longer automatically part of social groups that are looking out for us. We must make more effort to get support. Ironically, at a time when technology has removed many barriers to communication, our self-determination need of relatedness is often on thin ice. As we rely more on professionals to meet our human needs, we set higher and higher expectations of them. In turn, they set higher and higher expectations of themselves. Only a couple of generations ago, the main expectation of healthcare workers was to provide comfort and care; now it's to cure and prolong life. The world has been recently shocked by the graphic example of shifting expectations with the images of healthcare professionals being assaulted and abused for failing to prevent people from dying of COVID. As this expectation has grown in developed countries, so has the burden of often relatively intractable chronic disease. Many of the determinants of these chronic ailments are firmly social rather than biological. High technology may cure individual cancers, but reducing poverty, improving nutrition, reducing alcohol and tobacco intake, and cleaning up the environment are needed to reduce the burden of cancer. In my career, I have watched with increasing concern as politicians push the healthcare system to "get into prevention" with distressingly little insight that it needs a different skill set than frontline healthcare workers have. Not only is the expectation gap between healthcare workers and society growing but it's also spreading beyond the scope of their training. Talk about being set up to fail!

The original studies and applications of the MBI correlated the results with direct observations of the subjects and their stated intention to quit their jobs. The intended use was to "have practical benefit in recruitment, training and job design.[4]" It was never intended as a mental-health assessment or intervention. Indeed, the opposite end of the spectrum that the MBI was set to measure was workplace engagement, not mental health. Becoming burned out makes coming to work even more stressful. In 2019, The World Health Organization went as far as mentioning burnout in the ICD-11 classification of disease to specifically exclude it as a medical condition; WHO considers it an "occupational phenomenon."

There is certainly a relationship between burnout and defined mental-health disorders, but physician leaders should be wary of getting the two domains too tangled. Do we really need research-informed evidence of mental illness to work toward having a workplace that professionals enjoy, in which they can demonstrate their skills, enjoy the company and intellectual stimulation of talented peers, and feel in control of giving great care? And if we had such a workplace, would we not still need policy, process, and practices to support and accommodate colleagues with mental-health challenges? Physician leaders have a duty to seek both.

The Moral Injury Debate

Moral injury is the distress and/or impairment that we suffer when forced to witness or participate in events that offend our core values. A significant body of literature, particularly concerning war veterans, supports that trauma from Potentially Morally Injurious Events, such as a massacre or genocide, has different and potentially worse sequelae than those of morally neutral trauma, such as a natural disaster, and may warrant different interventions. There has been a strong dialogue, particularly in the United States, that the current perceived epidemic of healthcare professional burnout is entirely the stress of moral injury

---

4 Christina Maslach and Susan E. Jackson, "The Measurement of Experienced Burnout," *Journal of Occupational Behaviour*, 2(1981): 112.

imposed by a corrupt and dysfunctional healthcare system. A link to Dr. Zubin Damania's (ZDoggMD) frequently viewed YouTube video on the topic can be found in the "Further Reading" section. The more moderate position holds that any individual case of burnout will likely have both system and personal factors in play. Burnout due to one factor alone is improbable, but moral injury as one factor in most dimensions of healthcare is worth considering.

In an earlier chapter, the observation that we are hardwired for the value of fairness was noted. At one extreme, working within a system that provides care to individuals based solely on ability to pay, or a variation on that, and makes care choices based on profit, not patient benefit, will quickly cause moral injury. It is very easy for leaders working in public systems to look down their noses at private for-profit systems in such cases. But even in public systems, access is often unequal based on social status, education, and skill in playing systems. Any doctor or nurse working in those systems will tell you that. Conversely, the inverse relationship between health risk and socio-economic status for almost everything from physical trauma through to mental health, infectious disease, and cancer is seen every day by frontline workers. The rich get richer, and the poor get sicker.

Technology is also adding new layers of moral injury risk in any system. In many places, access to the newest, minimally invasive surgery techniques is economically restricted. As this book was being written, the development of a biological treatment to arrest the progress of Alzheimer's disease was announced. Like all monoclonal antibody treatments, it is seriously expensive. Even developed economies will struggle to make it available equitably. Where does that place those caring for these patients, seeing the evidence for the efficacy of such treatments but not being able to offer them? Can they truly divorce themselves from any sense of accountability for not offering what they may believe to be better care? Perhaps, for some, but I suggest perhaps not for most. Physician leaders need to recognize that some degree of moral injury is intrinsic to the territory in which we work. I don't believe it's possible to eliminate it, but there's much that social or corporate policy can do to make it worse. Support for the consequences of moral injury and strategies to mitigate it are properly part of a physician leader's mandate, or perhaps any leader's. A journey that starts in a local clinic may find itself in the world of advocacy for social justice.

Resilience and Burnout

Resilience is the ability to resist the negative effects of stress in your environment. Whereas publications applying the MBI burnout measurement abound and are proliferating uncontrollably, publications that actually measure resilience (versus just talking about it) are much harder to find. Resilience is a property we all possess to varying degrees. Advocates of promoting the development of resilience draw heavily on insights and practices of the Positive Psychology movement. They emphasize the importance of self awareness, self care, adopting positive perspectives, and recognizing one's own achievements and fostering optimism. A good overview of resilience-promoting interventions can be found in the article by Dr. Mark Stacey, who with psychologist Professor Andy McCann runs programs on this in the United Kingdom.

Resilience interventions by themselves certainly seem comfortably placed in the "primum non nocere (first do no harm)" category of things that can be tried. But physician leaders need to be cautious in promoting resilience as "the answer" to burnout. The evidence for these interventions as preventative or effective in mitigating burnout is not strong. To date, no systematic review, including a recent very detailed Cochrane review, has come out strongly promoting such an approach. Some are listed in the "Further Reading" section if you'd like to know more. As we will cover in a later section, organizational strategies that attack sources of stress directly seem to have more effect.

There is another real hazard for physician leaders in promoting resilience as the answer to burnout. Those embracing moral injury as a major influence in burnout see leading your burnout mitigation strategy with resilience training as victim blaming (with some justification). They see the message in such approaches as "You're burned out because you're not strong enough. Here are some exercises for you to get stronger." Once spoken out loud, this is a difficult genie to get back in its bottle.

This doesn't mean that resources to support resilience are a bad idea; it's just that the context in which they are introduced is critical. There's a certain level of unavoidable stress in healthcare, particularly mental-health, critical, and emergency care. People working in the most progressive and caring emergency department or urgent mental-health clinic may face unspeakable tragedies and horrors that can resonate in their own lives. They need and deserve support, including a nurturing of their resilience. This is just due recognition of their willingness to stand on that line, despite knowing what they will face. But once resilience training becomes proposed as the answer to poor scheduling practices, workplace abuse and harassment, poor resource allocation, unethical business practices, a blaming rather than quality improvement work culture, and lacklustre leadership, you are deservedly heading for trouble. Great leadership would confront these challenges head on.

Organizational Strategies to Reduce Burnout

Most physicians in developed countries now work in some sort of organizational structure rather than as individual solo practitioners. As time passes, more and more are salaried or working under time-based service contracts rather than as individual business owners. Many operate under the umbrella of university faculties. This contemporary reality means that viewing burnout only as an issue for individuals to manage themselves is outdated and short sighted. This phenomenon is costing organizations time, quality, and (if that's what drives your system) money. One study estimated that existing levels of physician burnout add US $7,600 per year to organizational budgets for every physician on the medical staff in the USA. The methodology for calculating that erred on the conservative side; the real figure could be higher. While one hopes that the moral imperative to look after one's people is enough to galvanize executive suites to act on this issue, there is a compelling business case.

The main locus of control that organizations have on this issue is their influence on the environment and culture in which healthcare is practised. Large private and public organizations may also have the ear of government and be able to use their skill and resources to advocate around resource and social-justice issues on behalf of those they serve. They have the potential to mitigate moral injury if they so choose. How this can be done is addressed in the final chapter of this book. The challenges and possibilities that each organization faces are their own, but several common features have been described in the literature. Cultural practices in healthcare organizations that can have a positive influence on managing burnout include:

- **Talk about it, but sincerely** - Physician leaders need to initiate conversations about this topic. But these need to be real dialogues where physician leaders demonstrate that they hear, understand, and are willing to act upon what is happening. On average, physician leaders can expect to find evidence of burnout in 40 to 50 percent of their medical staff. A common manifestation of that is cynicism, so leaders need to be prepared for a rough ride in entering this territory. These can be volatile conversations, and it can be challenging to maintain one's cool, but the payoff is huge if you can. The principle of acknowledging that everyone has their own experience, and that is their reality, is important to remember. This is a great example of the type of conversation that should be conducted by inquiring, not arguing.

- **Get the right people on the right seats on the right bus** - Everybody is different. Everybody finds meaning in their work in their own way. One of the most skilled interventions that organizations and physician leaders can do is this: Rather than just filling vacancies with people who meet the minimum requirement, cover those roles by aligning need with passion. Research outside of healthcare has emphasized the success of leaders who know their people and then fit them in the places where they will really enjoy the work.

- **Don't impose solutions** - The first problem with announcing a solution to burnout is that you are implying it's a problem that has developed. Solve it and we are done. Burnout is not a problem; it's a place in the workplace and professional landscape where, given the right circumstances, anybody can go at anytime. Managing the considerable challenges of healthcare while avoiding burning out yourself and your staff is a dilemma or conundrum that's present every single day. Managing the conundrum is a greater or lesser part of everything that happens in the organizational structure. If a satisfying, fulfilling career is the road you're on, burnout is the ditch running alongside it. Let your attention wander, and you may end up in the ditch. While there are some weaknesses in the literature, it seems that where approaches to stay out of the ditch have been developed and chosen at the grass roots level, and then supported and championed by leadership, impact may have been greater than where they were just imposed by executive fiat. This is a good area to apply quality improvement PDSA cycle methodology, where small changes are tested and gradually scaled up as promising results occur. Making expert resources available to support such a process is a valuable organizational contribution, as long it's done in the belief that the frontline professionals are the experts on their own experience.

- **Set a good example** - The obvious implication of this is for organizations to get their leaders to pursue fulfilling activities, show good wellbeing-maintaining behaviours, and demonstrate commitment to work-life balance. These things are nice but not the most important. The most important thing physician leaders can do is demonstrate vulnerability. They can be honest about their experiences, self-doubts, and when they need some time and space for their wellbeing. Their job is a to create a culture where being vulnerable is acceptable; the "physician as superhero" mythology and its consequences is covered later in this chapter.

- **Be consistent in what you reward** - Systems for remuneration, or even just performance/promotion review, need to be aligned with each other and with organizational and personal values. For example, can you imagine a system where someone's performance review in an area of complex chronic care is based heavily on patient experience surveys, but their remuneration is heavily linked to putting through large numbers of patients quickly? They exist. If you want quality, you need to reward and acknowledge quality.

- **Deal with the obvious** - Physician leaders need to be vigilant for behaviour and situations that are going to contribute to workplace stress or compromise the ability of those they lead to do their work to the standard they would like. Evidence of bullying or harassment, particularly where trainees are involved, must be addressed promptly and effectively. The final chapter of this book addresses ways in which physicians can wield influence for change; leaders need to engage early where there are problems and support physicians in skilled advocacy. They need to be seen to constructively use the influence they possess to work the system in the right direction. Mounting a campaign for change, even if progress is slow, can be a unifying and affirming experience. Certainly, getting the impression that one's leaders are not listening or don't care is not. It's also vitally important that organizations encourage and support their physician leaders to reach out to those showing any signs of distress.

As was discussed in the chapter on teams, bringing conflict into the open and creating traditions of working through it constructively is a necessary element in supporting people to mature the relationships in their teams and achieve their best. There are no human endeavours without conflict, but there are plenty where it never surfaces, or at least it never surfaces in the right place. One of the most toxic workplace cultures is one that is supported by a network of triangulation; everybody is griping about somebody to someone else, but no one ever tells anyone what they think to their face. Working in such a cave of whispering can rapidly become stressful and miserable.

In the chapter on meetings, I cited research from Google that being forced to attend meetings in which poor meeting behaviour was tolerated was the strongest driver of emotional exhaustion and disengagement. Organizations need to train and empower leaders to run great meetings and keep such behaviours in check.

- **Manage change skilfully and empathically** - System change, where it's perceived to be driven by values not shared by the affected healthcare professionals, can be very significant points in a journey to burnout. Obviously, you can't avoid change. But organizations can be transparent in communicating the change and the reasons for it. They can involve healthcare professionals in the change process while being honest about how much autonomy they do or do not have, and while providing clarity on how decisions will be made. They can mitigate known impacts of the change and have contingency plans to "expect the unexpected." Probably the best and most written about example is the introduction of electronic health records. A recent systematic review suggested that mitigating the stress and other negative impacts of electronic health-record introduction was the most effective among a suite of organizational interventions for burnout.

One of the critical things that organizations can do is stop subjecting talented clinicians to the "Peter Principle." This idea, articulated by education scholar Laurence J. Peter, is described in his own words: "In a hierarchy, every employee tends to rise to his level of incompetence."[5] Yes, clinicians and clinical leaders are all smart people, but they don't come preloaded with skills in human resources, accounting, and other corporate and business areas. Forcing them to master these on the fly while juggling their other work is common. This type of corporate behaviour is pulling them away from the type of work that gives them joy. Being forced to work in areas where one feels both unprepared and distanced from your core passion feeds performance anxiety. These are two very

---

5 Laurence J. Peter and Raymond Hull, *The Peter Principle* (New York: William Morrow & Company, Inc.,1969): 15.

effective steps toward burnout. Supporting them with skilled personnel and making training opportunities, *and paid time to do the training*, available to them are both simple interventions.

- **Destigmatize mental-health and counselling support** - It remains common for regulatory bodies to have different, and possibly coercive, standards around healthcare professionals who seek support for a mental-health concern. Not all burnout reaches the point of an identified mental-health diagnosis, but concern that you might be headed in that direction, or that if you express concerns about burnout, you will be assumed to have a mental-health problem may stop someone from making steps to change course. Does your practice or workplace accommodate someone working to overcome burnout, recover from alcohol or substance abuse, or deal with depression or anxiety with the same compassionate, confidential, evidenced-based approach as you would someone with a broken leg or recovering from myocardial infarction? If yes, great work! If no, physician leader, what are you going to do about it?

The Mayo Clinic had been something of a thought leader in organizational response to burnout. Their suite of nine strategies, listed in the article in the "Further Reading" section by Dr. Tait Shanafelt and Dr. John Noseworthy, is an excellent starting point for a more detailed exploration of this area. I have deliberately not made any structural organizational recommendations, such as hiring wellness officers and making lunchtime yoga classes available. If these are what people find helpful, they may be a good idea. They will, however, almost certainly fail if organizational and leadership commitment and action on culture change has not preceded their introduction.

Individual Strategies to Reduce Burnout

If we go back to the metaphor of a successful career path being the road, and burnout the ditch running alongside it, what will put you in the ditch? As someone who spends four or five months each year driving on snow-covered mountain roads, adverse local conditions causing you to lose sight of the highway, or traction upon it, is the first and obvious option for me. This is analogous to periods of stress and chaos such as we have seen with the COVID pandemic; it's no surprise that reports of burnout experience are increasing at this time. The road surface may be cracked and pot-holed so badly that you get bounced into the ditch. This is analogous to a poor working environment and poor leadership contributing to burnout. But even on smooth roads in clear weather, people sometimes end up in the ditch. They either lose focus and drift off course or miss the turn in the road. The former may occur when life and health circumstances change their experience of the type of work they're doing. The latter occurs when either the work changes, such as minimally invasive surgery replacing conventional open procedures, or the appeal of the work just declines with time. Even smart, talented people can get bored, or change their interests. Like the resilience issue, discussing the contribution of individual behaviours and decisions to burnout, and personal actions to mitigate it, can get push back as "victim blaming." But there's no way around it. Physicians and other highly independent professionals who battled through highly competitive systems to get to their current position are set up for burnout risk.

We've already touched on the high-risk nature of the work, and the increasing pressures as healthcare moves into larger and more technologically sophisticated systems. Another important factor is that, while we preach the importance of having a life outside of medicine, the reality for physicians, and indeed many professionals, is that the work has spread across the boundaries into our lives. This has a couple of broad manifestations. The most obvious is that, thanks to our wonderful connectivity, we can access patients' charts, organizational documents, and emails 24/7 ... and many do. In the chapter on time management, I pointed out that some industries and some European countries have legislated against this practice, but for most physicians in the English-speaking world, this intrusion persists.

The other way work creeps into physicians' personal lives is more insidious. There is general agreement that many factors, particularly in-hospital care, are crowding out any time for casual or opportunistic conversations between professionals. Most of the physicians I coach admit to bringing conundrums home and spending home time (or sleep time) turning them over in their minds. Almost without exception, these conundrums have not been discussed with a trusted colleague; coaching often becomes a discussion about how to create such an opportunity.

The final intrinsic burnout risk factor for physicians is the selection and training process. I touched upon this when discussing physicians and shame. One common behaviour to deal with shame is competence compulsion, where we construct stories about situations that always show that we are competent, whatever the actual outcome. Have you ever met a physician like that? If we're continually reframing the world in this way, it leaves little room to identify and address challenges, or seek help. Physicians are encouraged to perform to high (and at times ridiculous) standards, particularly in terms of continuous hours of work. Even now, surveys of medical students reveal that the "hidden curriculum" that rewards machismo and punishes complainers is alive and well. Dike Drummond, a former physician who now runs a very successful coaching organization that works with organizations exclusively in the area of burnout, notes that physicians are often their own fiercest critics. This leads to the creation of what he calls "physician head trash." This includes the concepts that physicians are "Lone Rangers" who can master any adversity alone, while being superheroes who can overcome any obstacle, no matter how large. Dike advocates that head trash needs to be put out for disposal as part of the journey away from burnout.

A comprehensive review of all the individual strategies that can be used to mitigate burnout is beyond the scope of a short chapter, and I would encourage you to dig into the "Further Reading." But I have been surreptitiously slipping a few in as we've been going along in this book. Having a clear vision of what you want to do and be, and developing logical steps to achieve it, is helpful. Reaching out and really engaging with colleagues is useful. Celebrating your personal successes and those of your team, rather than dwelling on what is yet to be done, is good. Taking pride in your competence and in increasing it is also a step in the right direction.

Identify the things that give you joy and the activities that put you into "flow," where time ceases. Then ensure those activities have pride of place in Quadrant 1 (urgent, important) and Quadrant 2 (non-urgent, important) of your Eisenhower time-management box. Ditto for those things that are important in your personal life. Dike Drummond describes this slightly differently and calls it "the calendar hack." For this, you create a powerful "single source of truth" calendar that has everything important in your life on it, both personal and professional.

There are quite a few studies on coaching and the use of mindfulness and other meditative techniques in physicians and nurses reporting burnout. Not surprisingly, these techniques have had many good reviews in support of some dimensions of stress management. Enthusiasm for them is considerable, and a coaching industry based specifically around this type of intervention is growing rapidly. Sarah Kriakous, Katie Elliott, Carolien Lamers, and Robin Owen recently conducted an extensive systematic review of research on Mindfulness Based Stress Reduction. This technique, developed and championed by Jon Kabat-Zinn, started as an approach to deal with stress in healthcare but has since been marketed much more widely. The analysis supported the technique as helpful in reducing individual experiences of anxiety, depression, and stress. They did not find, however, evidence that it improved burnout or resilience. Using the road and ditch analogy above, it helped with dealing with consequences of driving into the ditch, but it did not tow you out.

One aspect of professional life that can get enmeshed with burnout risk is money. As I mentioned in the chapter on motivation, money as an extrinsic reward has some problems. Where it replaces intrinsic motivation, research suggests that bigger and bigger "hits" of cash are required. It can become enmeshed with our perceptions of status and our identity. Yet research consistently shows that once income has reached a "satiation point," where it is sufficient to our essential material needs, further income does little for our happiness and wellbeing. The science, summarized in the article by Andrew Jebb, Louis Tay, Ed Diener, and Shigehiro Olshi in the "Further Reading" section, seems to suggest that while poverty is miserable, money cannot buy happiness. In both my medical leadership and coaching careers, I've seen physicians labelled as avaricious by their colleagues. While there were one or two true "Scrooges" in that mix, for most, money was a substitute for something missing. Those that broke the habit were invariably happier for it. Physician leaders should never accept financial motivation at face value; exploring why money is driving behaviour, whether in the context of burnout or negotiating service delivery or organization, is always worth the effort.

I believe there's another somewhat-sinister side to money, and more pointedly, debt, contributing to workplace stress and burnout for physicians and other healthcare professionals. It isn't unusual, in North America at least, for medical students to graduate with a level of unsecured, mid-range-interest debt that most people don't see until they buy a house. Medical students, residents, and to some extent other health-professional students and recent grads are seen as prime marketing opportunities for people in all sorts of financial services and luxury product industries due to their excellent possibility of long-term secure income. I'm aware of medical students who have been offered lines of credit comparable to what I have as a financially secure, forty-plus-year career professional. Skilled marketing professionals whisper in their ears of how much they are entitled to as a result of their hard and valuable work. Few have the luxury of coming from tough business backgrounds, and many are easy marks for this type of salesmanship. I've seen new consultants, fresh out of residency, not only having not paid off student loans but now having seven-figure mortgage and consumer debt. Once you're in a hole that big, the immediate demand for revenue seriously limits your work options.

The medical education system and all of us as a community of professionals need to do better in financial education. We need to avoid inadvertently feeding this monster by bragging about material acquisition or creating a climate in practices and workplaces where income is seen as a measure of personal value. On a positive note, while it's fashionable for my generation (Boomer) to trash talk millennials, my sense, supported by some data, is that the current generation are better than their predecessors at placing quality of life ahead of material gain. Maybe the ship is starting to turn in the right direction. But a lot could still be done to make that choice easier for them. The current system of starting healthcare careers in massive debt contributes to costs of burnout, and subsequently staff mental-health crises, low productivity, increased medical-error rates, leaving the profession, and discouragement of bright youth from minorities and socially disadvantaged groups entering healthcare. Looking through that lens, student-debt-elimination strategies no longer look like an expensive luxury. In many analyses, they are cheaper than the status quo. The costs of better financial and business education in professional schools are truly trivial; implementation just needs leadership.

Many of the approaches already put forward in other sections of this book have some research backing in terms of value in reducing the emotional exhaustion component of burnout, and to some extent, the other components. But there is some value to be had for physician leaders in confronting Depersonalization and Loss of Efficacy head on. The coaching component of my company is called "The Optimistic Doc," and there is, indeed, a story behind that. I frequently use the EQi 2.0 Leadership Report as an assessment for physician leadership clients. It measures fifteen emotional-intelligence competencies, but I was struck by how often I was seeing scores below the median for "Self Regard," which is like self esteem, and "Optimism." There are similar evidence-based practices to improve both, and I found myself regularly coaching them, hence the business name. I now encourage all leaders I coach to get a pen and a journal (research suggests that it doesn't work as well using a computer). I then ask them in private to record anything that they have achieved, big or small, work related or not; at the emotional level, your brain makes much less distinction about the size of an achievement than you might think. This simple exercise is a powerful reinforcement of self regard and a counter to Loss of Efficacy. It also can be used in public with other individuals, teams, or even organizations. At the same time, I ask that they record two or three things or people for which or for whom they're grateful. This has been shown to improve optimism. Improving optimism has positive roll-on effects with both Depersonalization and Loss of Efficacy. When in an optimistic frame of reference, we're more likely to see others in a positive light. We're also more likely to see adversity as temporary and circumstance-related. I encourage you to buy a nice-looking notebook and pen and give it a try.

Burnout mitigation is about keeping careers on tracks that are satisfying, sustainable, and sources of joy. It's everyday work, not a problem to be seen, diagnosed, and fixed. It's an area where coaching and mentorship can make valuable contributions, but not just by training in mental jujitsu. The role of coaching techniques in creating a safe space to reflect on career goals, organizational environments, personal choices, and areas for advocacy are where the real value is in the burnout domain.

The next evening, Rosalind gets a call …

"Hi, Rosalind, it's Derek."

"Hi, Derek, thanks for calling."

"I'm … I'm sorry it took so long to get back to you. I guess I'm causing you some headaches."

"You're certainly causing me some concern, not to mention Andy. What's happening?"

There was no reply for a bit, then, "I suppose everyone thinks I'm being a selfish jerk."

"No one knows what to think. All Andy and I have said is that you have an emergency to deal with. Everyone is respecting that for now. But Derek, Andy and I are really worried. What's going on?"

Again, a pause. "Remember that bad car crash outside of town a couple of weeks ago?"

Rosalind certainly does. A head-on collision between two pickup trucks at highway speed, one carrying a young family. Two adults and one child died, the child in the ER resuscitation room. Three others were seriously injured and required evacuation to the city. Derek had been in charge. They had to call in other doctors and nurses, but he had led the whole effort, and did so brilliantly.

"Not likely to forget it. Ever."

"Yeah … it was that sort of day. The next morning, I woke up, got up, and threw up as soon as I was awake enough to realize I had another day shift."

Rosalind is stunned. Derek had never shown any sign of not being well for as long as she could remember knowing him.

"But you came in that day. I saw you; you poked your head in when I was doing the trauma debrief."

"How could I not come in? People were depending on me. So, I hung in; I had three days off coming. I figured it would pass; maybe it was just some damn bug I'd picked up. But my next shift ... it was the same. And I was shaking in the car as I drove in. I got through the next four shifts feeling the same, had another three-day off spell, but I started feeling like crap on the day before my shift, so I went to see my GP. Nothing wrong physically. He basically gave me a choice: Take some time off now, or he might be forced to talk to the College."

"How long has this been going on, Derek? Surely not just the last two weeks."

Again, the pause. "I don't know ... each shift, they just seem the same, day in and day out. Same faces parading through ... same problems. I find myself starting to get angry with people for not taking enough care of themselves; then I have to work at keeping my mouth shut."

"So, what are you going to do?"

"Right now? We're going camping for a couple of weeks while I think about it. My GP wants me to call the Physician Health Program, but I'm worried the College will then come after me. Maybe there are some, I don't know, courses I can do for this stuff."

Rosalind had recently attended a webinar on the Physician Health Program activities. "No, Derek, they only have to report to the College if you're potentially a danger to patients or are actually hospitalized with a mental illness in this jurisdiction. I think the fact that you've voluntarily taken some leave speaks volumes to your insight about safety. They do have access to coaching and counselling programs that could help you figure out what to do."

"But what about here? What can we say to people here?"

"What do we have to say? You can ask for three months leave of absence without giving a reason, if supported by me and Andy, and we can just say you needed time off to deal with a private matter. You're entitled to privacy."

"Okay, let's do that then. Thanks."

"But Derek, I don't want you coming back to the same. We need to figure out what needs to change to work for you."

"That'll be tough with the number of shifts I do."

"But whose choice is that? I'm sure, between the others in the group, we can pick up a few shifts, and there are quite a few qualified people sniffing around for places to settle off the locum circuit. What about your teaching activities? You're so good at that. Maybe you could be doing more with that and fewer shifts. But let's not get too far ahead of ourselves. Take the time, but please keep in touch. And enjoy the camping trip."

"I will. That's a good thought about the teaching, I do enjoy that. I've had a few calls from the Rural Continuing Medical Education program about doing more with them, but it sort of felt like letting down the side if I'm cutting the clinical work. Let me think about it. I'll give you a call in a couple of weeks."

"Thanks, Derek, please do. Don't worry about the work—we can cover it. And do call the Physician Health Program."

Key Learnings

- *Understand that burnout is a work-environment issue and not a mental-health diagnosis; failure to mitigate or prevent burnout can, however, contribute to mental-health challenges.*

- *Burnout is not a problem to be solved once; it is always a possibility within all work environments if people lose sense of purpose, satisfaction, and meaning in their work.*

- *Be alert for circumstances that may place you or your followers at risk of moral injury, where they are confronted with something that deeply conflicts with their values. Such situations will accelerate disengagement from work and cause mental distress. Be prepared to support, speak out, and act in these circumstances.*

- *Encourage workplace wellness programs as valuable, but recognize that they alone will not rectify burnout, even if they reduce the symptoms or distress.*

- *Recognize that burnout is influenced by both personal choices and organizational policies and work environment; be prepared to address both.*

- *Focus on creating a workplace that maximizes sense of achievement, wellbeing, and purpose, rather than focusing on "fixing" burnout.*

- *Remember, leaders go first; set the best example you can of showing and managing your uncertainties and vulnerabilities.*

FURTHER READING

Burnout: History and Meaning

Christina Maslach and Wilmar B. Schaufeli, "Historical and Conceptual Development of Burnout," *Professional Burnout Recent Developments in Theory and Research*, eds., C. Maslach and W.B. Schaufeli (Abbington-on-Thames, UK: Routledge, 1993): 1–16.

Christina Maslach and Susan E. Jackson, "The Measurement of Experienced Burnout," *Journal of Occupational Behaviour,* 2(1981): 99–113.

Dike Drummond, *Stop Physician Burnout. When Working Harder Isn't Working* (Seattle, WA: Dike Drummond, 2014).

World Health Organization, "Burn-out an 'occupational phenomenon': International Classification of Diseases," May 28th, 2019, https://www.who.int/news/item/28-05-2019-burn-out-an-occupational-phenomenon-international-classification-of-diseases

The Moral Injury Debate

Zubin Damania, "It's Not Burnout, It's Moral Injury," July 1, 2021, https://www.youtube.com/watch?v=L_1PNZdHq6Q.

Brandon J. Griffin, Natalie Purcell, Kristine Burkman, Brett T. Litz, Craig J. Bryan, Martha Schmitz, Claudia Villierme, Jessica Walsh, and Shira Maguen, "Moral Injury: An Integrative Review," *Journal of Traumatic Stress,* 32(2019): 350–362.

Resilience and Burnout

Mark R.W. Stacey, "How to Be a Resilient Doctor: Skills to Maximize your Antifragility," *British Journal of Hospital Medicine,* 70 (2018): 704–707.

Carly Moorfield and Vicki Cope, "Interventions to Increase Resilience in Physicians: A Structured Literature Review," *Explore,* 16 (2020): 103–109.

Alex Pollock, Pauline Campbell, Joshua Cheyne, Julie Cowie, Bridget Davis, Jacqueline McCallum, Kris McGill, Andrew Elders, Suzanne Hagen, Doreen McClurg, Claire Torrens, and Margaret Maxwell, "Interventions to Support the Resilience and Mental Health of Frontline Health and Social Care

Professionals During and after a Disease Outbreak, Epidemic or Pandemic: A Mixed Methods Systematic Review," *Cochrane Database of Systematic Reviews,* 11 (2020): CD013779.

Organizational Strategies to Reduce Burnout

Shasha Han, Tait D. Shanafelt, Christine A. Sinsky, Karim M. Awad, Lisolette N. Dyrbye, Lynne C. Fiscus, Mickey Trockel, and Loel Goh, "Estimating the Attributable Cost of Physician Burnout in the United States," *Annals of Internal Medicine,* 170 (2019): 785–790.

Paul F. DeChant, Annabel Acs, Kyu B. Rhee, Talia S. Boulanger, Jane L. Snowdon, Michael A. Tutty, Christine A. Sinsky, and Kelly J. Thomas Craig, "Effect of Organization-Directed Workplace Interventions on Physician Burnout: A Systematic Review," *Mayo Clinic Proceedings, Innovation Quality Outcomes,* 3 (2019): 384–408.

Tait D. Shanafelt, John H. Noseworthy, "Executive Leadership and Physician Well-being: Nine Organizational Strategies to Promote Engagement and Reduce Burnout," *Mayo Clinic Proceedings,* 92 (2017): 129–146.

Individual Strategies to Reduce Burnout

Dike Drummond, *Stop Physician Burnout. When Working Harder Isn't Working* (Seattle, WA: Dike Drummond, 2014).

Jon Kabat-Zinn, *Wherever You Go There You Are. 10th Anniversary Edition* (New York, NY: Hachette, 2005).

Sarah Angela Kriakous, Katie Ann Elliott, Carolien Lamers, and Robin Owen, "The Effectiveness of Mindfulness-Based Stress Reduction on the Psychological Functioning of Healthcare Professionals: A Systematic Review," *Mindfulness,* 12 (2021): 1–28.

Andrew T. Jebb, Louis Tay, Ed Diener, and Shigehiro Olshi, "Happiness, Income Satiation, and Turning Points around the World," *Nature Human Behaviour,* 2 (2018): 33–38.

Canadian Federation of Medical Students, 2015. *Medical Student Loan Forgiveness*. Brief submitted to the House of Commons, Canada.

Robert A. Emmons and Michael E. McCullough, "Counting Blessing Versus Burdens: An Experimental Investigation of Gratitude and Subjective Well-Being in Daily Life," *Journal of Personality and Social Psychology,* 84, Issue 2 (2003): 377–389.

WHEN DO I GET TO CHANGE THE WORLD?

Chris, the Chief of Staff, comes into the hospital cafeteria. She spots Sanjay sitting at one of the tables, with one of the general surgeons standing over him. While voices aren't raised, the surgeon is gesticulating and does not look happy. If Sanjay leans any further back in his chair, he'll be on the floor. She buys her lunch and goes over to them. By the time she arrives, Sanjay is alone again, now staring into space.

"May I join you?" she asks.

Sanjay jumps. "I'm sorry, Chris. I was somewhere else. Yes, of course, please sit down."

"That looked like quite the ding dong you were having with our surgical colleague."

Sanjay sighs. "You can say that again. All I did was mention how keen we were to recruit some gastroenterologists, and he went ballistic. I know the general surgeons do all our gastroscopies and colonoscopies, but we have a lot of other gastro service gaps that are forcing patients to go outside our watershed to get care. But he just thought I wanted to put them out of business!"

Chris nods. "The surgeons are pretty sensitive about anything that might cut into their procedure time, if you'll forgive the pun."

Sanjay continues. "My department really wants to set up a real gastroenterology call schedule. It's not just about bread-and-butter elective scopes. We have a lot of people with liver disease, Crohn's, and pancreatic issues that need specialist support. We have physicians with no formal training writing parenteral nutrition orders all over the hospital. In a lot of cases,

those patients don't even need it, but our dietitians don't have any special-
ist back up when they suggest cheaper and safer enteral feeding. A proper
gastroenterology service could fix all that. And now I'm told the surgeons
will do everything they can to block it, just to protect their incomes."

Chris shrugs. "That's one interpretation, and one that I would say is a
bit simplistic and harsh. We do still certainly need general surgeons, but
the impact of better medical therapy, minimally invasive and day surgery
procedures, and frankly, competition from other specialities such as gastro-
enterology and radiology doing more procedural work, has put them in an
increasingly tough place."

Sanjay's blood is up. "But none of those things are new, and they should
have been planning for them. Why should we hold up progress in quality of
care to spare their feelings? Don't you have the authority to just tell them
this is the direction we're going and to just suck it up?"

Chris smiles. "I could do that, but I don't think you'd like the outcome,
unless guerrilla warfare is something you enjoy. Force people to do some-
thing, and they'll invest huge amounts of time and effort in finding ways not
to do it. Trust me, docs can be really creative in that department. I'm willing
to work with you on this, and you need to know I agree with you—we need
that service. I think most of the medical staff would also agree. But that
doesn't mean they will pick your side if you make this a conflict with surgery.
So, let's see if you can start a campaign for this change that doesn't involve
antagonizing the surgeons. I'm going to send you a couple of articles on stuff
around driving change that I want you to read in the next week— they're
short. Then let's meet and see what ideas you have."

At the beginning of this book, I suggested that most physicians move into leadership because they want to make a difference. This chapter is written using an assumption that physician leaders don't merely want to induce any change for the sake of it—they wish to innovate to improve healthcare. Innovation in complex human systems needs to engage and understand the people who will be involved. It needs power to shift from the current state and drive the change. Above all, it needs a plan. This chapter examines some important concepts around leading for change.

Picking the Target

One of the keys to success in influence for innovation is to select the right people to influence. Physicians are well educated and articulate. They often come from lived experience that makes them confident in dealing with organizations and individuals. In situations where feelings are running high, the urge to go straight to "the person in charge" can be overwhelming. Too often, however, this is more about who the physician thinks should oversee the issue that's on their mind than who really is in charge. Missing the target can have serious consequences. Shooting too high, like approaching a Minister of Health about a parking spot issue, produces at best puzzlement and at worst annoyance in someone whose longer-term goodwill would be valuable. Going under the correct target is no better. Haranguing someone who has no authority to address the issue will achieve nothing toward a positive outcome. They may not be able to make the decision wanted, but there's a good chance that, if upset enough, they'll use their communication channels to sabotage the effort. At worst, it might earn the physician a harassment complaint. Whether missing high or low, poor choice of target leads to wasted time.

Physician leaders need to educate themselves about how the system in which they practise works. All systems have their own unique nuances. For any issue, physician leaders must explore the pathway through which necessary decisions are made. Sometimes, they're not the obvious ones; curiosity is an asset here. There are some general characteristics of healthcare systems, however, that at least suggest where the starting points for those explorations should be. These are summarized in Table 4. Someone, or some group, has accountability for the overall vision of the system and the decisions that affect all parts of it. This level is the place to take big ideas, not small or local challenges. Understanding the priorities of this group is necessary, to some degree, for innovations at all levels of the system. While an innovation that aligns with the system-wide priorities will have other hurdles to clear, one that opposes them may be dead in the water. Often the difference is not so much real but an issue with how the innovation was presented. Not making the effort to explore how an innovation aligns with these priorities tends to result in it being treated as if it does not. There's no substitute for doing your homework.

If this senior level decides what will be done, the next level of senior and mid-level leaders at a regional, large program or large-facility level tend to decide where it will be done, and to some extent, how. This level is often attracted to innovations that increase value for the money the system spends and quality projects that are ready to move out of single-unit experimentation. The level of autonomy varies widely between different systems, but issues about what is being done where, policies that manage common processes and workplace behaviour, and how budget follows patient care are mostly made at this level. These people tend to be at the sharp end of the stick for resource decisions. Physician leaders are well advised to understand the conundrums these leaders face and to explore ways to present their innovations as solutions.

Finally, there's a level where day-to-day decisions and patient care occur. This level is the place to launch basic quality initiatives that need a few cycles of tweaking to test ideas, or simple innovations that meet a local need. At whatever level an innovation inserts into the system, it will be judged by its impact on the frontline. This level is all about the how. Following policy is important, but these levels need the autonomy to adapt to individual local circumstances. They are the stewards of information that exist nowhere else.

Table 4.

Organizational Level	Example	Priorities and Decisions
High-level governance and policy	Public—Ministry of Health Private—Multinational or Multistate Health Care Corporation, Hospital, or Clinic Chain	Overall system priorities and finance System-wide risk Major capital projects Board and senior leadership appointments System-wide bargaining and contracts
Service delivery organization	Public—Regional health authority Multisite hospital and/or clinic system Private—Hospital or clinic grouping, large complex of facilities	Location of specific services Management of workforce and facilities Professional regulation and governance Minor capital projects Community relations System quality Recruitment strategy
Program or facility	Community or smaller hospital Individual metropolitan or small rural program Individual clinics	Day-to-day operations Patient scheduling Patient-care planning Staff scheduling Individual staff performance Recruitment Local site issues (e.g., fire safety, parking)

Levels of Organization in Typical Healthcare Systems

Physician leaders need this frontline level as an ally in almost all innovations. Physician leaders, by virtue of their clinical role, are well placed to have strong relationships here. They need to look after them.

Another dimension of targeting innovation in healthcare is timing in budget and/or planning cycles. Most healthcare organizations, public or private, operate on some form of fiscal cycle. There are, of course, deep differences between public systems that are charged with maximizing value while controlling cost, not-for-profits that must balance revenue generation against value and costs, and for-profits that must maintain quality to be competitive while producing a return for shareholders. But all will have a cycle that moves from alignment to new priorities, through assessing progress and adjusting the course, to evaluating their position and planning the next phase (Figure 9). As a rule, innovations that require some investment and carry a certain risk need to appear on the organizational radar early in that cycle. This is when the organization needs to find ways to move toward new goals and may have an appetite for some risk in doing so. Conversely, late in the cycle, when the system may be straining to come in on budget or hit a financial target, such an innovation may not get a friendly reception. But sometimes an innovation requires a tough decision to stop doing something else. The late cycle environment may be the perfect time to make that move.

Figure 9. Typical Organizational Budget and Planning Cycle

People and Innovation

In 1962, American sociologist Everett Rogers published *Diffusion of Innovation*. The book went through several editions before his death, and Rogers' theories remain a dominant force in thinking about how innovation occurs within groups and organizations. Rogers identified four major elements within an innovation process that influence the uptake within a population, each of which have their own factors that influence the speed and success of adopting an innovation. These are shown in Figure 10.

- **The Innovation** - Relative advantage requires the demonstration of benefit compared to the current state. Physician leaders need to recognize that this may look different to people in different parts of the system, such as the internists and surgeons in Sanjay's conundrum. Compatibility certainly applies to technological issues but also may need to include human factors such as values and beliefs. Technology that is more efficient but seen to be diminishing or eliminating work of a cherished staff member may not be seen as compatible. Complexity refers to whether the innovation is easy to both understand and apply. Trialability refers to how easily people can test it for themselves. This is an important way to both preserve autonomy and reduce anxiety generated by uncertainty. If people cannot resolve their doubts about an innovation, the resultant anxiety will guarantee the dominance of negative stories about it. Observability is simply how visible the innovation is. Adoption is more likely when the people being asked to adopt it can see it at work in similar environments. Physician leaders wanting to bring in change should always be on the alert for such opportunities. All these five characteristics are in the eye of the beholder. Success is more likely if the information is framed based on how those that need to adopt the innovation see these properties.

  Communication - The way in which information flows about an innovation has a strong influence on its rate of adoption. One consistent feature in research in this area is that whoever the potential innovation adopters trust is more powerful than the quality of technical information and data from manufacturers and sales forces. The physician leader responsible for innovation needs to know how trusted people can be recruited to support the cause.

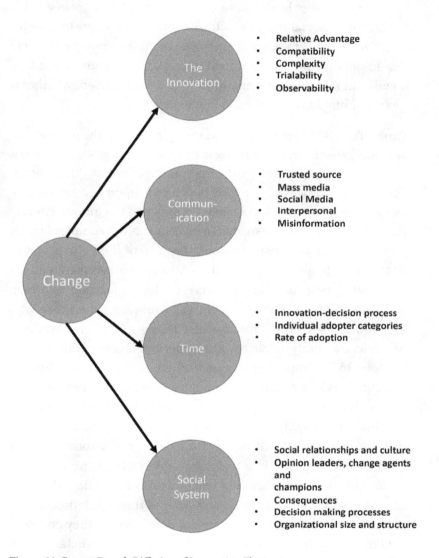

Figure 10. Everett Roger's Diffusion of Innovation Theory

A twenty-first-century variation on this theme is the impact of misinformation. When Rogers wrote his book, the ability of individuals to directly access and create mass communication without any need for accuracy or veracity hadn't developed to the level it has today. The wise leader has a contingency to be aware of what is being said on social media about their project and how to counter misinformation. Physician leaders responsible for major projects should plan for professional help in this area. The one thing that is constant about misinformation is that it will happen, whether it spreads around the office water cooler or via Twitter.

- **Time** - Time is in turn divided into three categories: the innovation-decision process, adopter categories (which is arguably the most famous aspect of Rogers' work), and rate of adoption. The innovation-decision process is in turn dependent upon several factors, including when the adopter becomes aware of the innovation and when they start to be persuaded in its favour. More complex factors play into organizational decisions that are beyond the scope of this review. Rogers proposed that Adopter categories could be represented by a bell-shaped curve of the population at which the innovation is targeted (Figure 11). Innovators are those who will embrace something just because it's new. They are extremely risk tolerant. Early adopters also embrace change without fear but tend to be more circumspect and measured in their decision making. They're not difficult to persuade with a reasonable case but won't try something just for the sake of it. The early majority, who make up roughly one third of the population, will adopt faster than the average but will usually have developed a good rationale for their decision. The late majority, a group about the same size as the early majority, will adopt when options to not do so become limited or risky. Finally, about one-sixth of the population can be expected to be laggards, who may not adopt ever. If they do adopt the innovation, it's with great and often very vocal reluctance, and only when there's no other choice. Where people sit on this curve can vary according to which innovation is being brought forward. A famous chef might be a radical innovator in terms of recipes and use of ingredients but a laggard when it comes to culinary tools and technology.

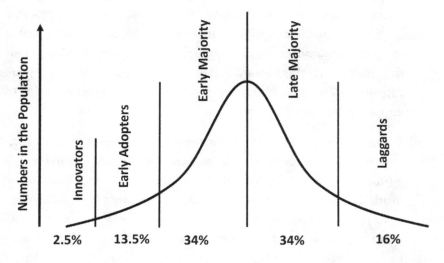

Figure 11. *The Rogers Innovation-Diffusion Curve*

When an innovation is proposed, often the most noise comes from the laggards. This has several hazards for the physician leader proposing the innovation. It may obscure the true level of support for the innovation, as the innovators, early adopters, and early majority who make up half the population are rarely as vocal. The leader can expend huge amounts of effort and energy trying to convince the laggards, who are beyond persuasion. But ignoring the laggards is equally risky. Their hostility to the innovation means they may see risks more clearly than innovators. Problems can also occur if a leader only consults with other innovators at the other end of the spectrum. The leader and their organization may be lulled into a false sense of security as to both the readiness of the environment and the population to accept the innovation. The other important component of time is the rate of adoption. The rate of adoption follows an S-shaped curve with a gradual onset. This is then followed by a period of relatively rapid adoption as the innovation moves through the early then late majorities. Finally, adoption slows again as the laggards reluctantly come on board. This can also present problems for the innovative physician leader, particularly if the innovation is one that requires skilled technical support. Success will mean being able to keep the support resources at a level that is just ahead of the rate of adoption. Invest in too much support too soon and your support units will be twiddling their thumbs and wasting money. Fail to invest enough to meet the peak rate of adoption and your innovation will stall. The people trying to adopt will become frustrated and hostile to your innovation.

- **Social Systems** - Social systems form the container within which a given innovation or change occurs. In the physician leader's world, it could be as small as a single unit or clinic or as large as the World Health Organization. How the social system is organized can have powerful influences on how an innovation spreads. Whether control is centralized in the hands of a few (inhibits innovation) or is diffused among teams (facilitates innovation) is an important influence. Complex systems with wide ranges of skills and expertise in their members are more innovative and accepting of change. On the other hand, large formal systems that place high value on adhering to rules tend to be less innovative. Systems with high levels of interpersonal connection between their members are more innovative. If not bound by the excessive constraints of rules and formality, larger organizations can allocate more resources to innovation and are better able to support a long game as the innovation moves across the spectrum from innovators to laggards.

There are important roles within social systems that are necessary for change and innovation. Opinion or thought leaders are members of an organization who are respected for their wisdom and whose word goes a long way to supporting an innovation. Change agents are usually people from outside the group who bring specialized knowledge and problem-solving ability to support the change. Perhaps the most important role for any major innovation is that of the champion. Champions are drawn from the population who must adopt the change. They're usually innovators or early adopters, but they also have strong interpersonal relation-ships within the group and are widely respected by it. Identifying and recruiting these people to an innovation effort is an early and essential priority for leaders.

Understanding the people who must adopt an innovation is as impor-tant (or more so) than deep technical knowledge of the innovation itself. Within that understanding, the physician leader must recognize that the members of any group, large or small, will have divergent positions on their readiness to accept an innovation. Starting from an assumption that one size will not fit all and having a range of strategies for different levels of innovation readiness is more work at the start but likely to be less effort in the long run.

Power and Innovation

In the natural world, change occurs because of work, meaning the dis-placement by force of objects from the size of subatomic particles to gal-axies. The rate at which work happens and changes occur is expressed as power, which is the amount of work achieved per unit of time. In human systems, the idea of power as the potential available to influence events probably best captures the thought behind the word.

Power is a word that has taken on some negative connotations. The word has become entangled with issues of discrimination and bullying and harassment in the workplace, community, and even between nations. Physician leaders need to be quite specific in their meaning when they talk of power and the use of power. A useful framework considering the use of power comes from the work of sociologists John Raven and Bertram French. In 1959, they categorized corporate or organizational power into five types, although the model has now been expanded to six. These fall into two categories: positional power and personal power. Positional power includes coercive power, reward power, and legitimate power. Personal power includes referent power, information power, and expert power.

The category of power is particularly important in the discussion of using power for change. Positional power is largely independent of any relationship between the person wielding the power and those who are subject to it. Those on the receiving end adopt a desired behaviour to avoid a sanction or receive a reward. Once the task is done and the penalty avoided or award received, their attitude to the task will likely be unchanged from prior to being asked to perform it. They can take it or leave it. Positional power makes people comply. It doesn't need to care how they feel about complying. That compliance will last only if power continues to be applied. Ongoing coercion may breed resentment that may stir people to rebel openly, or do so via stalling or even sabotage. The threat of ever greater sanctions may become necessary as resistance hardens.

As I mentioned earlier, using reward to secure compliance can lose its potency over time. Legitimate power that rests in the authority conferred on a position in a hierarchy may use a combination of both carrot and stick, although the wise leader builds personal power use into their legitimate role. To sustain change using positional power alone, more and more coercion or reward may be required, until it becomes unsustainable and collapses. There are many examples of this in the natural history of authoritarian-leadership situations. In short, positional power is not much help in driving innovation. Innovation feeds on enthusiasm and imagination, not just compliance.

Personal power, on the other hand, is highly dependent on some relationship between the person wielding power and those on whom it is wielded. Most successful leaders often get their best results with personal power. They use the authority of their position only as a backstop and in times of crisis. The outcome of the use of personal power is uncertain. Unlike positional power, which primarily acts on behaviour, personal power primarily acts upon motivation. With the use of personal power, people's behaviour aligns with the desired goal because they want to do so, not because they must do so. When an innovation is adopted as a free choice, it's reasonable to expect that the change will be sustained. Successful innovation depends on effective use of personal power.

An important concept in thinking about types of power is to recognize that there is no overall right or wrong type of power. The art of wielding types of power is in selecting the best type of power for specific circumstances. For example:

- **Coercive Power** - The power to punish is clearly not one on which to build relationships. An appropriate use might be cancelling operative privileges for a surgeon who refuses to follow the pre-operative checklist protocol. Allowing the behaviour to continue would put patient safety at risk, which clearly outweighs the risk of generating bad feelings. An inappropriate use would be requiring a student or resident to work outside of stipulated conditions or do tasks beyond their scope under threat of a bad assessment or withholding a reference. An abuse of this power that sometimes tempts physician leaders is the "Embarrass them into action!" ploy. This is where a story of crisis in healthcare is put into the public view without any warning to senior leaders or politicians. The intent is to force action by putting them in an untenable position. While there may be circumstances that warrant extreme advocacy, doing this in advance of efforts to get the system on side is likely to backfire in the long term. Politicians have long memories and often are not forgiving. The damage done to not only the physician leader's future influence but also that of their colleagues and the institutions in which they work can be considerable.

- **Reward Power** - Providing some form of extrinsic gratification for behaviour is still an important basis of our economic system; we pay people to come to work. Offering extra reward for one-time unusual tasks, or as an unexpected gesture for extraordinary effort, is an appropriate way to use this power. Buying pizza for the busy ER or ICU, or flowers or a dinner voucher for a unit clerk who provides service above and beyond, are good uses of reward power. Using it alone for sustained change is not appropriate. Neurophysiology determines that bigger and bigger rewards will likely be required to sustain ongoing change. One example that keeps coming up in the Canadian context is using cash incentives to promote recruitment and retention of rural physicians. Lump sums may get them in the door, but many iterations of these programs have failed to support retention. Interestingly, research examining physicians who did stay in rural environments revealed retention was driven by intrinsic motivation factors. These were strongly aligned with the principles of self-determination theory, competence, relatedness, and autonomy, and were largely independent of money.

- **Legitimate Power** - This is the form of power that comes closest to the concept of authority. This is power vested in an organizational position. The line between legitimate and the other forms of positional power can be a fine one. Defiance of legitimate power can be reasonably expected to attract sanctions. Compliance may permit continued accumulation of benefits. Physician leaders are given the right to impose their will in specific environments on a specific range of issues. A Chief of Staff deciding on scheduling for a service that cannot seem to agree on this would be an appropriate use of legitimate power. A department head, with accountability for physician performance, using his position to critique the performance of a nurse in a specialized unit who reports in a different line would be an inappropriate use of legitimate power. In the current environment, such behaviour is a common cause of harassment complaints. A department head passing on objective concerns to that nurse's manager would be appropriate use of legitimate power.

- **Referent Power** - This is the power that comes from being known, respected, or liked. This is the process in play in the phenomenon of celebrity endorsements. People are likely to align with your innovation as a way of being more connected to you. The Canadian Women's Hockey legend Hayley Wickenheiser entered medicine after her hockey career and parlayed her fame into advocacy around the challenges facing the Canadian healthcare system early in the COVID-19 pandemic. This is a very appropriate use of referent power. The most insidious and inappropriate use of referent power is the "old boy's network," versions of which are sadly found everywhere. These are situations in which individuals have influence that is often quite covert, based upon who they know and to which groups they belong, not their skills, knowledge, values, or achievements. Patterns where such groups work to protect their own interests at the expense of people closer to the front line, or the organization and those it serves, are common.

- **Information Power** - This is power achieved by providing and being seen as a source of reliable information. The driving force behind change is the persuasive information you provide. Dr. Najma Ahmed, a Toronto area trauma surgeon and tireless advocate for safer gun laws, has been highly effective in communicating her experience in dealing with the victims of gun violence to support the case for legislative action. Her only authority in this matter is the credibility of her information and the way she delivers it. While coercive power is a bad way to deal with politicians and senior leaders, information power that aligns an innovation as a solution to challenges those leaders face is an excellent approach. At the other extreme, one of the most egregious abuses of information power was the fallacious results published by Dr. Andrew Wakefield that fueled the still widely held belief that vaccines cause autism. This tragic example underscores the ability of the application of personal power to generate change that sticks, even if we would prefer it did not.

- **Expert Power** - This shares some features with both referent and information power but is the power that comes when people respect you as the expert in the issue at hand and are willing to proceed on trust of your word. It needs a relationship that has been built to a high level of trust. It often develops after a period of conscientious and successful application of information power. In the saga of the COVID-19 pandemic, Dr. Anthony Fauci, who throughout 2020 was consistently seen in many circles as more trustworthy than the president he served, is a good example of expert power on display. His past extensive contributions to the understanding of the HIV/AIDS epidemic have appropriately conferred expert status with respect to patterns of infectious disease spread. Abuse of expert power is most commonly manifest as "scope creep." A person abusing this power will try to lever knowledge or expertise in one area into giving the impression they have comparable expertise in another. Obviously, straightforward impersonation of an expert would count as such abuse. Access to information over the Internet and better record keeping in most professional bodies is making that somewhat more difficult to do.

It's common when coaching physician leaders to hear a lament about the lack of power. Physician leaders pine for the power to say, "Make it so!" Senior leaders, however, often reflect that having even the authority of the VP Medicine or CEO is not enough to drive change by itself. Physicians and physician leaders are, in fact, immensely powerful, but rarely from position. Study after study shows that for all the skepticism toward modern medicine we see in social media, the general population place more trust in the credibility of physicians than almost any other group. The challenge is for physicians to tap into the personal power they hold as respected members of the community (referent), well-informed and well-educated individuals (information), and as authorities in their fields (expert), and let go of trying to change things by force.

Planning for Innovation

Just as teams in human social systems have their own developmental history, so does change. Change management has become a recognized discipline. Introducing largescale innovations in healthcare is now commonly supported by teams of such professionals. The smaller incremental changes that support real-time quality improvement in patient care, or the experience of providers at the front line, still require that physician leaders master the basic principles and skills for change.

One of the oldest models of change is Kurt Lewin's three-step process of change that dates to 1947. Lewin suggested three change steps: *unfreezing*, where people who must adopt a change admit that their previous beliefs no longer match the circumstances; followed by *changing* to new beliefs, which then *freeze* again into a new, stable equilibrium. A similar idea comes from William Bridges, whose three phases are "Ending," where someone bids farewell to the old state and then moves to a "Neutral Zone," a somewhat uncomfortable place of limbo between the old and new, before they enter the "New Beginning," where they regain their sense of comfort as they adopt new behaviours.

Reviewing models of change does tend to recall the Indian parable of blind men describing an elephant; each model seems to focus on one aspect more than others. Elizabeth Kübler-Ross' stage theory describes the emotional states that people subject to change may pass through as they move to adopt change (denial, anger, bargaining, depression, acceptance). William Howell is popularly credited with a model that focuses on four stages of new skill development: unconscious incompetence, conscious incompetence, conscious competence, and unconscious competence. Peter Senge, author of the influential book *The Fifth Discipline*, and Richard Boyzatis, who described the Action-Reflection cycle, emphasized the dynamic nature of change as an ongoing process that creates feedback that drives further change. This is like the Plan Do Study Act (PDSA) cycle of quality improvement. While useful in understanding change, these models are less helpful in making a practical road map for change. Two models that do offer more practical advice are the eight-step model of John Kotter, and the six sources of influence within the Influencer© model from the Crucial Learning (formerly Vitalsmarts) organization, originally authored in 2008 by Kerry Patterson, Joseph Grenny, David Maxfield, Ron McMillan, and Al Switzler.

Kotter's model has three phases. The first phase, involving the first three of the eight steps, creates a climate for change and could correspond to "unfreezing" the system. The second phase, involving the next three steps, engages and enables the group to get into the innovation. The final two steps consolidate the change, essentially "refreezing" the system. The steps, with examples drawn from Sanjay's project to start a gastroenterology unit, are described below:

- **Create urgency** - Sanjay needs to create some helpful anxiety to move people away from the current system. He could gather statistics on wait times for service for patients who cannot access a gastroenterologist at his hospital. He could collect compelling stories of hardship, where patients have had to travel for care. He may be able to access quality data that shows less than optimal outcomes of certain classes of patients that might have been better with this type of support. Alternatively, he may be able to show that there is a manpower crunch coming in this field, and if they don't recruit soon, the competition for such specialists may be even more fierce. Are there people currently supporting these patients as a side interest who are considering dropping this service or retiring? If he needs higher-level support, he needs to show that his innovation of creating the gastroenterology group solves an issue for the larger system, such as meeting targets for cancer-screening procedures.

- **Assemble a guiding team** - This is where Sanjay needs to be thinking about his social system and identifying thought leaders, change agents, and champions. His thought leaders could be drawn from existing senior members of the medical staff. Change agents might be someone like a gastroenterologist already working in a similar environment who can advise on the best way to set up such a group. A champion might be a surgeon at the site who believes that they could work in harmony with gastroenterologists. Setting up a new service will impact other services and have resource implications for the hospital. Sanjay needs to engage administration, ambulatory clinics, and surgeons to help develop strategy to overcome resistance to the change and create a welcoming and supportive environment for the new specialists. If there are battles to be fought, they need to be over before a recruit appears. Sanjay may want to consider reaching out to someone in the community, like a realtor with experience supporting executive or professional moves, to help show the community in its best light as a place to live. This also may be a place to look for support from patient-advocacy groups, like the local chapter of a Crohn's and Colitis Foundation, for example.

Sanjay needs to be careful that his guiding team reflects a diversity of views so that, collectively, they cover each other's blind spots.

- **Have a clear vision** - While creating urgency tends to play on fears and anxiety, creating a vision is looking at the other side of the coin. Sanjay needs to be able to describe a strong, positive image of how his department and the hospital will look with a strong, high-functioning team of gastroenterologists on site. What procedures will be possible that are not possible now? What onerous tasks can be moved from other over-stretched individuals? What outcomes will be better? Sanjay would be wise to test the vision as it's being developed with groups likely to be affected by the change, including not just physicians but other staff and departments that will find themselves involved in supporting the new activities. Their feedback should be used to refine it and make it as inclusive as possible. This vision is essential to maintain support for the new program in the hospital and attract high-quality recruits. It also can be useful in reassuring the larger organization that the change aligns with higher priorities.

- **Communicate for buy in** - Sanjay needs to understand the range of opinions and concerns that exist about this project. He needs to harness his best listening skills before he speaks. He then needs to work with his thought leaders, change agents, and champions to communicate the vision in a way that addresses the concerns that are arising. They will encounter everything from enthusiasm to anger and must be prepared for all. This communication needs to be a dialogue, not a sales pitch. Sanjay would do well to identify settings where he can start giving periodic updates and receive new ideas and feedback. Examples might be a Medical Advisory Committee, Hospital Manager's Group, or the regular department meetings of the departments closest to the change. If he needs high-level support, he should try to get an opportunity to present to the senior leadership team or board.

- **Enable or empower action** - As the project picks up pace, things will begin to happen in recruitment, in the organization of clinical services, in the procurement of equipment, etc. Sanjay must confer some autonomy to his team members to problem solve and be creative on these fronts. Managing this aspect of the change calls upon him to use the delegation skills he has recently acquired, as he remembers that conferring autonomy is an important part of keeping people motivated!

- **Create short-term wins** - Sanjay needs to sustain belief in the possibility and value of the innovation he's trying to create. One way of looking for short-term wins is to listen to the failure points that the cynics will invariably produce for you, for example, "You'll never get the space for more endoscopy." This creates the opportunity to celebrate a win when the organization agrees that more space should be found. "No one is going to come here and be the first member of the group." This creates a short-term win opportunity when a way is found of supporting someone as the lone specialist while the group grows, and another win when applications and expressions of interest come in. Then you move on to the first recruitment, the first clinic, the first performance of a new procedure, and so on. It may feel a bit like marketing or theatre, and perhaps it is, but it's vital to keep the innovation moving.

- **Build momentum** - While building a series of milestones that become your short-term wins is important, keeping focus on the original vision and being sensitive to any stalling of forward progress is critical. Sanjay needs to think about which specific gastroenterology skills he needs most and first, but he must keep working toward group-level resources and multiple recruitments. Any obstacles that appear must be handled without any procrastination, particularly once recruitment has started. Credibility and trust in a leader depend in part on getting results. Once the process is underway, the system, and particularly the first recruits, will be looking to Sanjay to complete the process. Alternatively, everybody wants to ride on the fastest train, and the sense that this project is going somewhere will help sustain support.

- **Affirm the new culture** - Sanjay needs to ensure that the vision isn't just a paper exercise but is something that comes into existence. Successes must be celebrated and the new way of doing things emphasized, underscored, and promoted until any other way of operating is a dim memory. Never assume successes speak for themselves louder than older, more established cultures.

The Influencer© model, which is described in detail in the book of the same name, proposes a two-by-three matrix that creates six sources of change or innovation activity. An example of applying this to the physician-leadership environment can be found in the "Further Reading" section in the paper by Snell, Eagle, and Van Aerde. The columns are motivation and ability, with rows being personal, social, and structural. Each cell of the matrix contains a process necessary to support change or innovation (Table 5).

Table 5.

	Motivation	Ability
Personal	*Make the undesirable desirable*	*Surpass your limits*
Social	*Harness peer pressure*	*Find strength in numbers*
Structural	*Design rewards and demand accountability*	*Change the environment*

The Six Sources of Influence in The Influencer© Model

If we apply this to Sanjay's situation, the six sources come out something like this:

- **Personal motivation—make the undesirable desirable** - Sanjay has two targets here. On the one hand, he needs to convince hospital administration and the medical staff that this is a good idea. On the other hand, he needs to convince gastroenterologists that setting up practice at a site that has never supported such a service before is desirable. With the medical staff, he needs to make the

213

case that the risks of any competition over patients and procedures will be minimized by increased and different service demands. He may need to find credible ways of reassuring people that they will not involuntarily lose space or procedural time, or he should find fair alternatives if that *will* happen. He needs to be transparent with hospital administration about resource demands but build a good case for value that offsets those demands. His approach will combine some of the elements in the eight-step Kotter model that are used to create urgency with strong positive vision. The vision forms the core of his approach to making this desirable to the gastroenterologists he hopes to recruit. He needs to align his approach with the principles of self-determination that was covered in an earlier chapter. He must make a credible case to them that they will be able to practise to the full scope of their training, that they will be part of a supportive medical community, and that they will have control over their practice and lives. If he needs some big things to make it happen, he needs to be ready to make it desirable to senior leadership by showing it will help achieve system-wide goals.

- **Personal ability—surpass your limits** - The focus in this section is the individuals carrying the change: the gastroenterologists Sanjay succeeds in recruiting. We will put the technical or equipment considerations aside for now (they are considered in another source). Are the people available for recruitment comfortable working alone in a small group, particularly if they are recent graduates from a large tertiary program? Do they have the skills to develop the interprofessional relationships they'll need to be members of a small, tight-knit medical community? Would they benefit from having local or regional mentors? Sanjay needs to have answers and strategies prepared for these questions.

- **Social motivation—harness peer pressure** - Sanjay knows that the other internists, and many of the family practitioners attached to the hospital and working in the community, would love to have a gastroenterology service locally to accept patients who are now either travelling for care or being managed by physicians who are less than comfortable with some of the issues they are facing. But he has surgeons who are worried about losing scope time and income, and a hospital administration that is juggling competing priorities. He needs to get his colleagues to support the cause, not by haranguing those less enthused but by keeping their compelling stories of need out in the open.

- **Social ability—find strength in numbers** - This is about finding allies and partners. Sanjay getting time to present to the Medical Advisory Committee and perhaps the hospital board on why they need a gastroenterology service would certainly be a good thing. Now imagine the impact if that presentation was followed by a compelling supporting presentation from a prominent member of the local community on behalf of a coalition of patient-advocacy groups. The hospital foundation or other fundraising groups may be induced to offer matching funding support. Sanjay could also seek support from a local medical school to create a community resident or medical-student rotation in gastroenterology in exchange for an automatic university appointment for his recruits. Coming to his community hospital effortlessly retains ties to a potential academic career, making the position more attractive to those wanting to retain such ties.

- **Structural motivation—design rewards and demand accountability** - Sanjay again has two dimensions he must manage. He needs to ensure the system will support the gastroenterologists, hopefully not at too great an expense to other physicians currently working in the system. He has also made commitments to the medical staff and hospital administration that this new service will deliver value worth at least the time, money, and effort put into setting up the service. He needs to make reasonable efforts that arriving gastroenterologists can expect levels of referrals from his colleagues that will allow them to get off to a good financial start. He also needs to identify metrics that will reassure everyone that the service is living up to expectations. These could include waiting-list statistics for consults and procedures, detection rates of intestinal cancers and cancer-surgery avoidance, changes in numbers of referred out gastroenterology procedures, or patient satisfaction data.

- **Structural ability—change the environment** - Adding a service like this will almost certainly require changes to the physical environment in the form of additional equipment and procedural space. It may require additional services in the form of nursing, pharmacy, and anesthesia support for procedures. It may require the creation and funding support of new on-call groups or services. Specialized nursing roles might be needed that in turn require new training and scope of practice policy. Addition of highly specialized procedures may require certification by an external regulatory body. Sanjay needs to anticipate all of these and work with the right people to find solutions. As much as possible of this should be done prior to recruitment, unless it's possible to support a recruit in doing some of this themselves. This would mean not only moral support for them as new leaders but also financial support for both their time and potential lost income while their scope of practice is restricted by factors other than their credentials and experience.

Meanwhile, Sanjay has been getting some tips from Chris. We pick up the conversation a couple of weeks later ...

Chris stops Sanjay in the corridor. "How's the planning for your gastro recruitments going?"

"Actually, better. Thanks. I took your advice and talked to the surgery department head, who was a bit more sympathetic. They're concerned about being muscled out of endoscopy, but part of that is due to limitations on the amount of minimally invasive surgery they can do. They feel we need another OR set up for laparoscopic surgery. He actually has some data on how far behind we are on meeting our quota of screening endoscopies for the cancer program, so he didn't see the amount of work as a problem. It's going to be about how we share resources."

"Did you get anywhere on that?"

"Sort of. It's pretty clear we're going to need more time and space for scopes if this is to work. We're wondering if we might be better creating a

compelling vision that ties all the needs together. Something like modernizing care for the twenty-first century, or moving to care that gets people back into the community faster. We could then go to the Board and fundraising, suggesting that both the OR changes and increased scope resources are needed. There are some other things we need to probably factor in as well. For example, if we can hire gastroenterologists who have advanced training for pancreatic procedures, that will impact radiology as well. We may need to look at some changes in fluoroscopy. We're pulling together a bit of a group from the relevant departments to see if we can come up with a strategy to take to senior leadership that we can all live with."

"Sounds promising. What about potential recruits?"

"Well, we have had a couple of inquiries from people in training. I'm keeping them in the loop of what we'd like to do and where we're at. I'm a bit worried they may not be too keen if they see we're still just setting up, but I'm also concerned that if we give the impression that we're more ready for them than we really are, that could blow up in our face."

"Very wise. But don't underestimate the potential benefit of being in on the ground floor of setting up something new. I'd suggest you make it a two-way conversation and get their thoughts on what would work. I'd also suggest you get some input from some other gastroenterologists, even if they're not potential recruits. I can reach out through the Chief of Staff grapevine to find some names for you if you like."

"That would be really helpful, thanks."

"Let's put this on the agenda of the next Medical Advisory Committee. It's never too soon to start getting people thinking about a big change like this. You might find a few other people willing to help."

Key Learnings

- *Understand the structure and function of the organization that you want to change; pick your targets carefully.*

- *Know the decision, finance, and planning cycle of the organization you want to change and pick the time to move that best fits the intention of your change.*

- *For any innovation, be ready to show its advantage, ensure it is compatible with existing systems and culture or have a plan to make it so, and create opportunities for observation and testing.*

- *Have an intentional communication approach that is built on the culture of the organization you want to change.*

- *Understand the population who must accept the change; recognize that there will be a spectrum ranging from enthusiasm to absolute resistance and have a flexible approach to deal with this variation.*

- *Be prepared to use power to drive change but understand there are different types of power. Positional power may produce compliance, but lasting change requires the use of personal power to change the motivation of the people who must accept the change. This requires time to develop relationships and trust.*

- *Change needs a plan. Use one of several models of change that can help you identify and structure tasks that must be accomplished to achieve change.*

FURTHER READING

People and Innovation

Everett M. Rogers, *Diffusion of innovations* (Cheney, WA: Free Press, 2003).

Jennifer P. Lundblad, "A Review and Critique of Rogers' Diffusion of Innovation Theory as It Applies to Organizations," *Organization Development Journal*, 21 (2003): 50–64.

Power and Innovation

John R.P. French Jr, and Bertram Raven, "The Bases of Social Power," in *Studies in Social Power*, ed., D. Cartwright (Ann Arbor, MI: University of Michigan, 1959): 150–167.

Anurag Saxena, Diane Meschino, Lara Hazelton, Ming-Ka Chan, David A. Benrimoh, Anne Matlow, Deepak Dath, and Jamiu Busari, "Power and Physician Leadership," *BMJ Leader*, 3(2019): 92–98.

Planning for Innovation

Robert James Campbell, "Change Management in Health Care," *The Health Care Manager*, 27 (2008): 23–39.

Anita Joanne Snell, Chris Eagle, and John Emile Van Aerde, "Embedding Physician Leadership Development within Health Organizations," *Leadership in Health Services*, 27 (2014): 330–342.

Joseph Grenny, Kerry Patterson, David Maxfield, Ron McMillan, and Al Switzler, *Influencer: The New Science of Leading Change* (2nd edition) (New York, NY: McGraw-Hill Education, 2013).

LAST WORD

I hope this book has given you some useful information to help you plan your leadership journey. You now have some understanding of concepts and terms you may not have previously considered. I hope you're feeling better prepared for some of the situations in which you find yourself involved. I'd like to think you're now starting to look for more and deeper details on some of the topics lightly touched on here. Thank you for hanging in there and getting to the end!

By now you've seen quite a list of other books that contain ideas you'll find helpful on specific elements of your leadership experience. In the chapter on change, I mentioned Kurt Lewin's model of change that describes an initial step of "unfreezing." Sometimes it's necessary to unfreeze your ideas of what leadership is before you can make progress. This is particularly true if your personal experience of leadership has been of the brash, ego-driven "my way or the highway" type. I suggest a couple of books that use research-based evidence to demolish old leadership stereotypes. The first is *First, Break All the Rules* by Marcus Buckingham and Curt Coffman (New York, NY: Simon and Schuster, 1999), which describes conclusions about the relationship between beliefs and practices of managers and employees and indices of business success. It was drawn by researchers at the Gallup Corporation from a massive metanalysis of their corporate research data. This work was the foundation for their twelve-step program for employee engagement. The second is *Good to Great* by Jim Collins (New York, NY: HarperCollins, 2001), which explores leadership and strategy in Fortune 500 companies that substantially outperformed their sector in the index. I have found the insights in this book particularly useful in helping medical research groups and organizations refine focus and develop strategy.

Much as I appreciate you reading this book, I must leave you with the final piece of advice. Please do not try to do leadership just from books! Valuable as they are for introducing you to many useful, and some awesome, ideas, physician leadership is best developed as an apprenticeship, like medicine itself. Find leaders you can respect and admire. Connect with them, study them, even critique them—if they are worthy of your admiration, they'll be fine with all that. But also look for strength in numbers. Connect with others on the same or a similar journey. Do this informally within your organization. Look for regional physician-leadership-development programs, or national physician-leadership associations. Watch for meetings, courses, and online groups. Consider leadership-development groups outside of medicine. LinkedIn is a great resource to research what's out there.

Physicians and other high-performing professionals with technical or scientific backgrounds tend to love using analytical tools and instruments. It may surprise you that I have been quite sparing in referencing leadership assessments and similar tools. As this is a book that is designed as an introductory survival guide, this is a choice, not an omission. As a coach, I do use several such tools. They're like laboratory tests and imaging studies in medicine; before you order them, you need to know what you'll do with the information they generate. I certainly have clients who come to me having already done Myers-Briggs, EQi, Enneagram, Strengthfinders, or other such assessments with some course and program. Without a relationship with someone who will help them debrief the analysis and integrate the findings into their leadership vision, without exception, there has been nothing produced from having done such assessments. They are great tools, but only when there's an appropriate context in which to use them.

Another apparent omission may seem to be a discussion about emotional intelligence. Here I must confess to being somewhat subversive. You will notice that I've been quite forthright in several sections about the importance of acknowledging emotion, both your own and that of your followers, and factoring that into your leadership. That, in a nutshell, is emotional intelligence. Many of the strategies and tactics suggested in this book are firmly rooted in emotional-intelligence-based approaches to coaching and leadership development. If you're interested in learning more about this, Daniel Goleman's popular books, *Emotional Intelligence* (New York, NY: Bantam, 1995, 2006 10th Anniversary Edition) and *Social Intelligence* (New York, NY: Bantam, 2006) are good places to start. Consider doing an emotional intelligence assessment; there are a number of scientifically validated tools that can be accessed through human resource departments and appropriately certified coaches.

This leads me to coaching, a word that has cropped up a lot in this book. A large part of the reason I coach now is that I wish I'd had access to coaching much earlier in my career. Physician organizations have been a bit slow to come to the coaching party compared to other sectors of developed economies, but better late than never. Please remember that coaching is not about fixing problems. It assumes that the person/people being coached are capable, competent, and complete. It's about helping them explore ways to be the best they can be. Individual coaching is powerful, but new physician leaders are often great candidates for group coaching. In group coaching, they combine the insights of coaching with the power and connection of peer wisdom, and often at a lower cost to themselves or a sponsoring organization. I hope you will explore what coaching can offer you.

Enjoy the journey!

Dr. Malcolm Ogborn, MBBS, FRCPC, COC, PCC
The Optimistic Doc,
www.optimisticdoc.com
Kelowna, BC, Canada
November 2021

ACKNOWLEDGEMENTS

The idea for this book has been floating around for a long time. As a result, it has been shaped in some way by many people. Looking back from the most recent to more remote past, Liza Weppenaar and the publishing team at FriesenPress are the most recent influence. They have taken much of the angst out of turning a whole lot of words into an actual book, while being kind and considerate to a first-time author. My colleagues in the Canadian Physician Coaches Network, ICF BC Interior Chapter, and the Clear Leadership Network have not only reassured me that this effort is worth doing but also kept me moving by asking about the progress! Special mention is due to Dr Johny Van Aerde whose insightful critique made the important opening chapters much stronger.

The year spent working with the Organizational Coaching Program at the University of British Columbia in 2017 taught me that there is always another book you need to read to keep up in coaching and leadership; those books pushed me to fill a need for one that really spoke to physicians and other self-directed professionals. The biggest influences on the content of this book, however, are the many physicians, nurses, midwives, health administrators, leadership-development program directors, and students who have allowed me the privilege of entering their lives through coaching, mentoring, or seminars. It has been a pleasure and an honour to share their experience, absorb their wisdom, and walk with them while we figured out what works and what doesn't. If they find this book useful, it is a success.

None of this would have happened if my own thinking about leadership had not been elevated at some point. I think every leader with whom

I have worked, and there have been many in my gypsy-like career, has influenced me in some way, large or small. Credit for the epiphany that leadership skills are not automatic and that there is a rich body of knowledge to be mined to help develop them is due to some of my early instructors in the Physician Management Institute (now Physician Leadership Institute), particularly Monica Olsen and Linda Tarrant. They flicked the switch that started me applying the type of intellectual rigour that I used in research and clinical work to leadership. Elevated thinking alone does not perfect practice make; the many, many stumbles along the way and those who took me to task for them have also shaped what you have read.

Finally, this would not have been possible if my wife, Jane, had not encouraged the idea, and been gracious about the amount of our (semi) retirement time it has eaten, kind in keeping the morning coffee and afternoon tea flowing during the writing process, and ruthless and accurate in her proofreading.

INDEX

Note that the italicized letter following the page reference relates to a figure ("*f*"), or a footnote ("*n*"), or a table ("*t*").

CPSIA information can be obtained
at www.ICGtesting.com
Printed in the USA
BVHW061456050422
633412BV00002B/111